RECORDED VERSIONS GUITAR

AUTHENTIC TRANSCRIPTIONS WITH NOTES AND TABLATURE

PAT METHENY – UNITY BAND

Lead sheets by Pat Metheny
Music transcriptions by Masa Takahashi and Pete Billmann

As a bonus, the actual lead sheets used in the recording session have been supplied by Pat. The harmonic analysis (key signatures, time signatures, chord symbols and enharmonic spellings) presented in the transcriptions that follow represent the overall harmony of the ensemble, and do not necessarily always match the symbols in Pat's original lead sheets.

ISBN 978-1-4803-4038-1

HAL•LEONARD®
CORPORATION
7777 W. BLUEMOUND RD. P.O. BOX 13819 MILWAUKEE, WI 53213

Visit Hal Leonard Online at
www.halleonard.com

New Year

By Pat Metheny

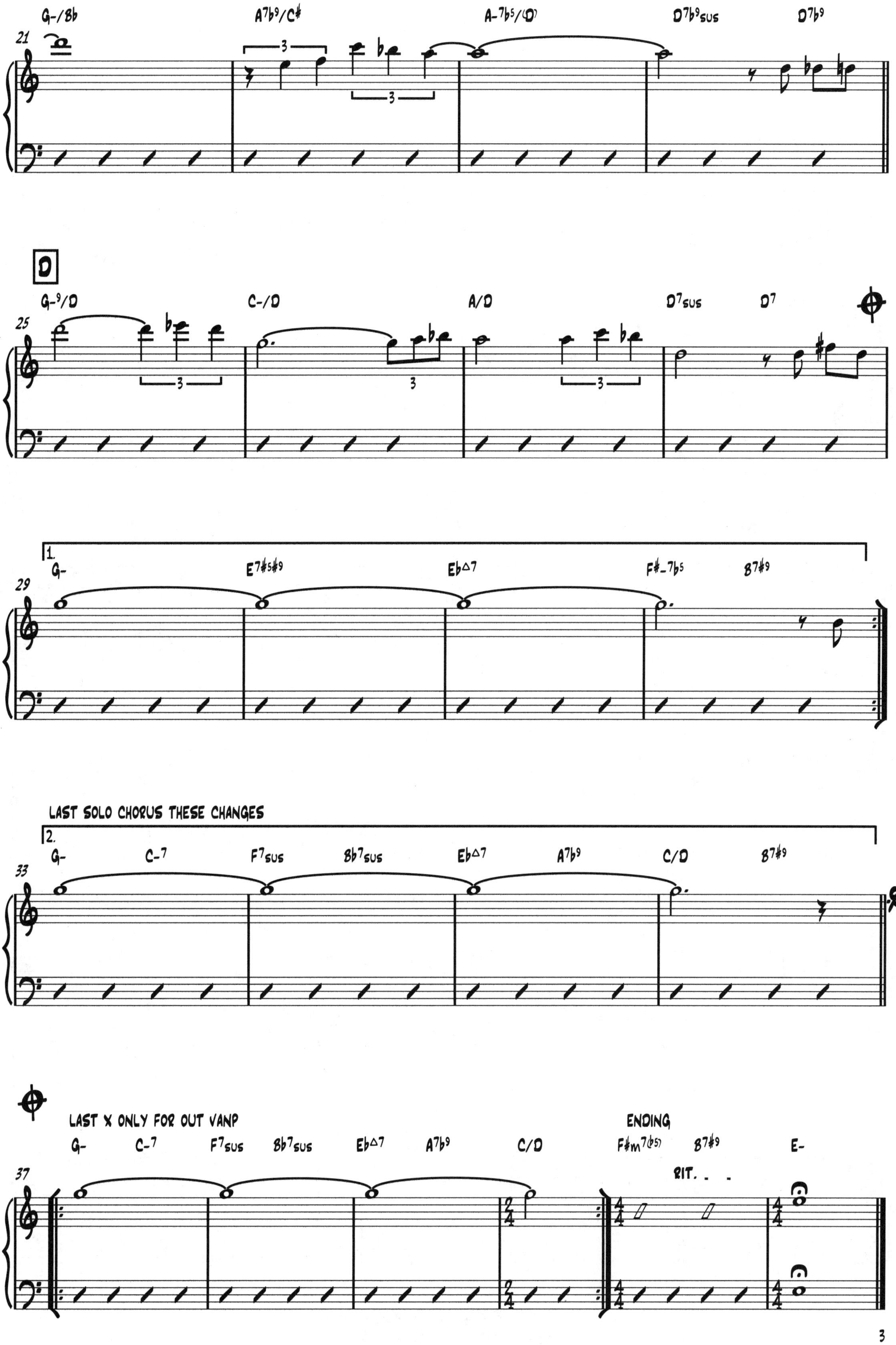
G-/Bb
A7b9/C#
A-7b5/(D)
D7b9sus
D7b9
D
G-9/D
C-/D
A/D
D7sus
D7
1.
G-
E7#5#9
Eb△7
F#-7b5
B7#9
LAST SOLO CHORUS THESE CHANGES
2.
G-
C-7
F7sus
Bb7sus
Eb△7
A7b9
C/D
B7#9
LAST X ONLY FOR OUT VAMP
ENDING
G-
C-7
F7sus
Bb7sus
Eb△7
A7b9
C/D
F#m7(b5)
B7#9
E-
RIT. . .

Roofdogs

By Pat Metheny

36
E-
1
E
2
A7sus
A7sus
8
A7sus
F
14
F△7♭5
B7
G
22
E-
A-7
C△7
E-
28
H
E-
A-7
C△7
34
F△7♭5

Come and See

By Pat Metheny

D
21
Gbsus
Fbsus
D△7
Fbsus
E
29
Gbsus
Fbsus
D△7
F
TO CODA LAST X
37
Db-
42
G
SOLOS
Db-
47
D/Db
G/Db
51
Db-
H
Db-
D/Db

56
G/Db
Db-
I
61
Gbsus
Fbsus
D△7
Fbsus
69
Gbsus
Fbsus
D△7
2
2
J
77
Db-
81
K
BASS SOLO
85
A-
D-
A-
Bb△7b5

1.
2.
L
93
A-
G-
F△7
Gsus
Absus
102
Db-
106
BACK TO A
THEN TAKE
CODA
110
Db-
114
Db-
Db-
120
Db-

This Belongs to You

By Pat Metheny

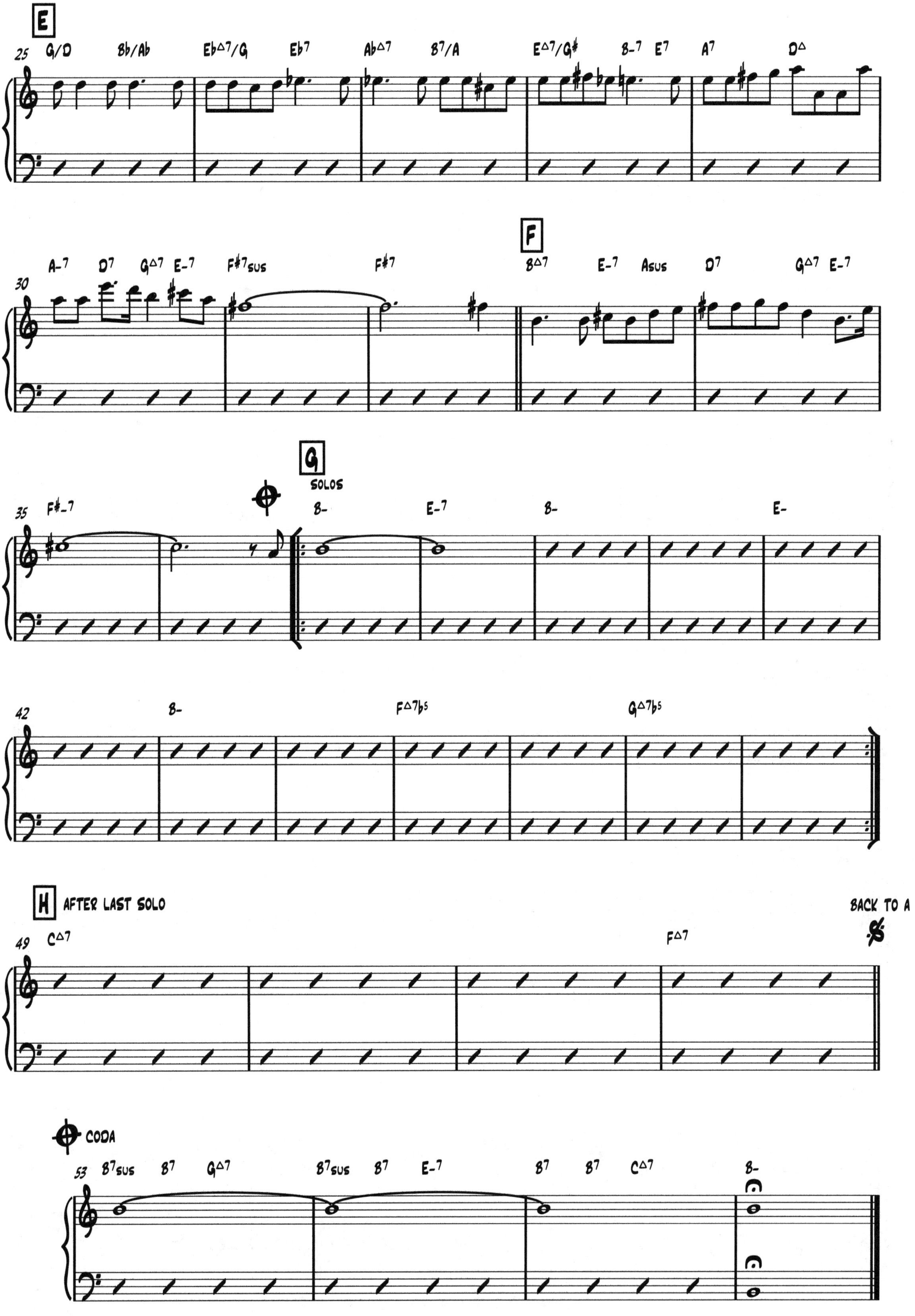
E
25 G/D Bb/Ab Eb△7/G Eb7 Ab△7 B7/A E△7/G# B-7 E7 A7 D△
30 A-7 D7 G△7 E-7 F#7sus F#7
F
B△7 E-7 Asus D7 G△7 E-7
35 F#-7
G
SOLOS
B- E-7 B- E-
42 B- F△7b5 G△7b5
H AFTER LAST SOLO
BACK TO A
49 C△7 F△7
CODA
53 B7sus B7 G△7 B7sus B7 E-7 B7 B7 C△7 B-

Leaving Town

By Pat Metheny

LAST TIME
19
Ab
Bb/C
F
Db
21
Ab
Eb
Bb
Csus
E
24
Db△7
Bb-7
C7sus
Db△7
Bb-7
Eb7
Ab△7
B/Db
F
29
B/Db
D/E
Ab/A
D/E
Asus
Db/D
Gsus
B/C
33
F7sus
A/Bb
Eb7sus
D7sus
G
37
C/D
G
F△7
G/B
F
BADD9/D#

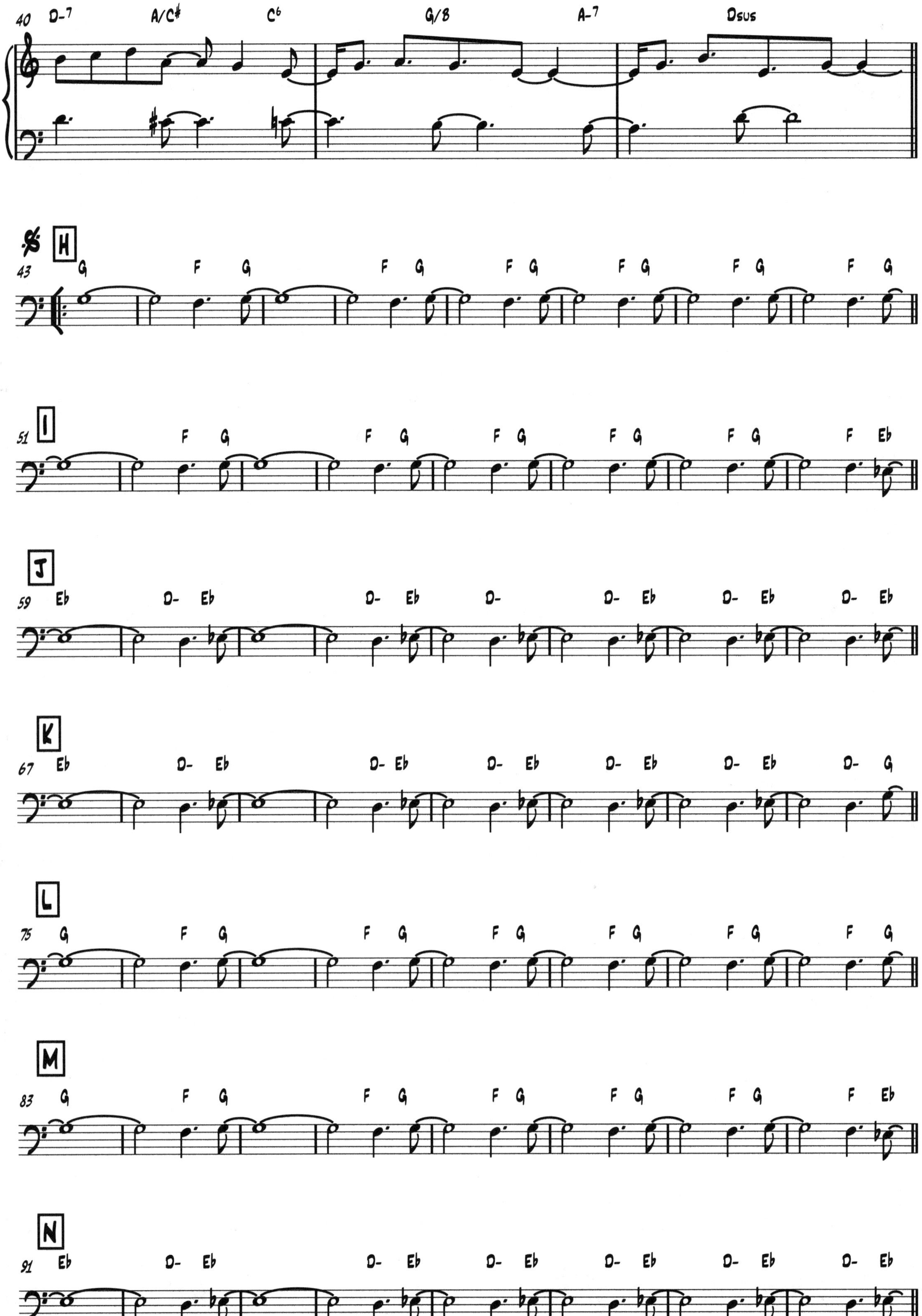
40 D-7 A/C♯ C6 G/B A-7 Dsus
H
43 G F G F G F G F G F G F G
I
51 F G F G F G F G F G F Eb
J
59 Eb D- Eb D- Eb D- D- Eb D- Eb D- Eb
K
67 Eb D- Eb D- Eb D- Eb D- Eb D- Eb D- G
L
75 G F G F G F G F G F G F G
M
83 G F G F G F G F G F G F Eb
N
91 Eb D- Eb D- Eb D- Eb D- Eb D- Eb D- Eb

O
99 Eb D- Eb D- Eb D- Eb D- Eb D- Eb D- C
P
107 C Bb C Bb C Bb C Bb C Bb C Bb
Q
115 A- B-7 C△7 B-7 A-7 B-7 C△7 B-7 A-7 B-7 C△7 D
AFTER 2ND SOLO
GO TO CODA 1
R
BETWEEN SOLOS
123 C/D G F△7 G/B F BADD9/D#
126 D-7 A/C# C6 G/B A-7 DSUS
BACK TO H
FOR NEXT
SOLO
CODA 1 AFTER 2ND SOLO BEFORE OUT HEAD
129 G F G F G

133
F G G F G F
BACK TO TOP FOR OUT HEAD
CODA 2 - FROM OUT HEAD
137
Ab Eb
S
Db/Eb Ab B/Db
140
Gb△7
T
Bb/C F Eb△7 F/A Eb AADD9/C#
144
C-7 G/B Bb6 F/A G-7 Csus Db
U
147
Db△7 B△7 Gb△7 F

Signals

(Orchestrion Sketch)

By Pat Metheny

Interval Waltz

By Pat Metheny

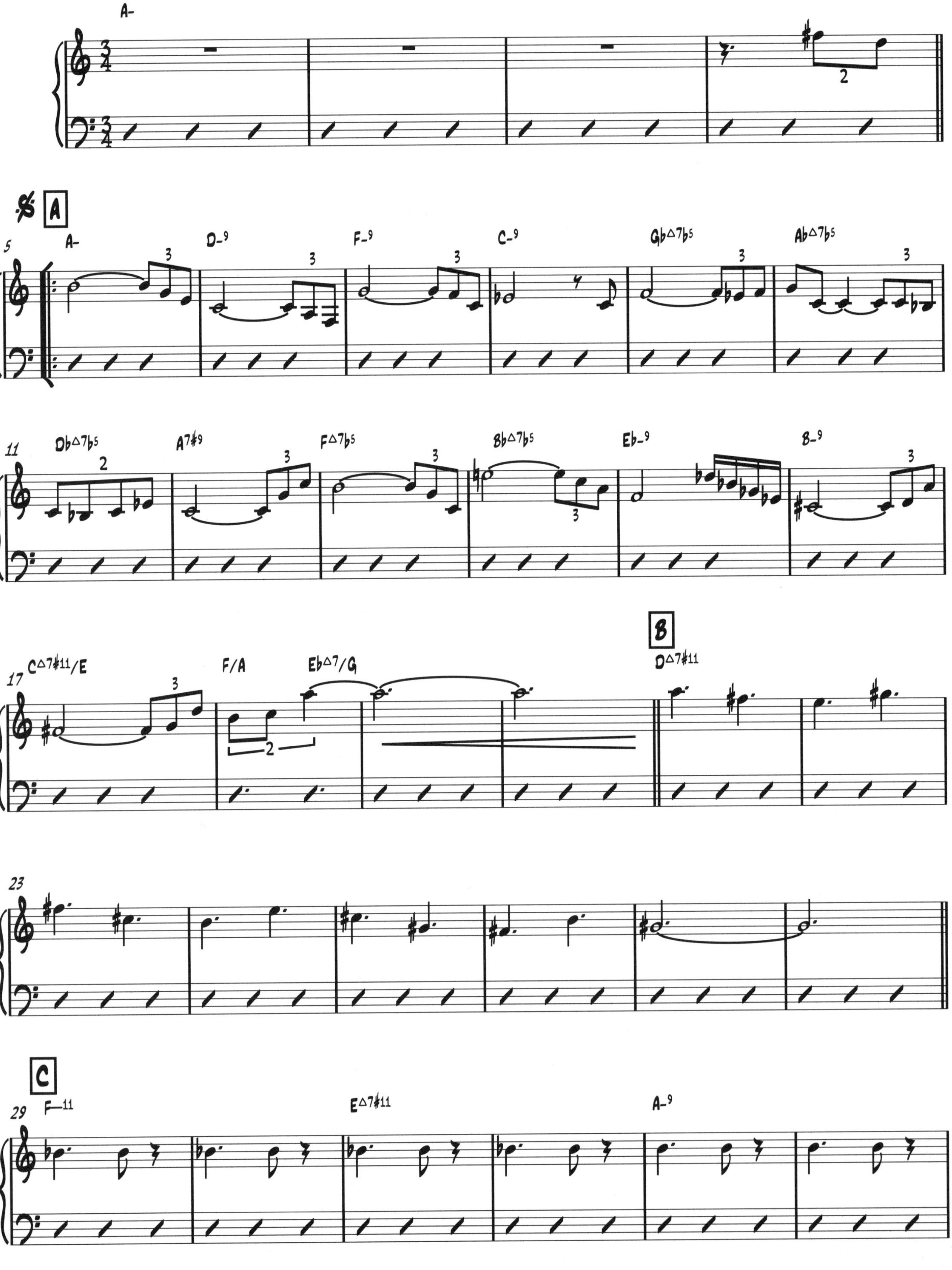

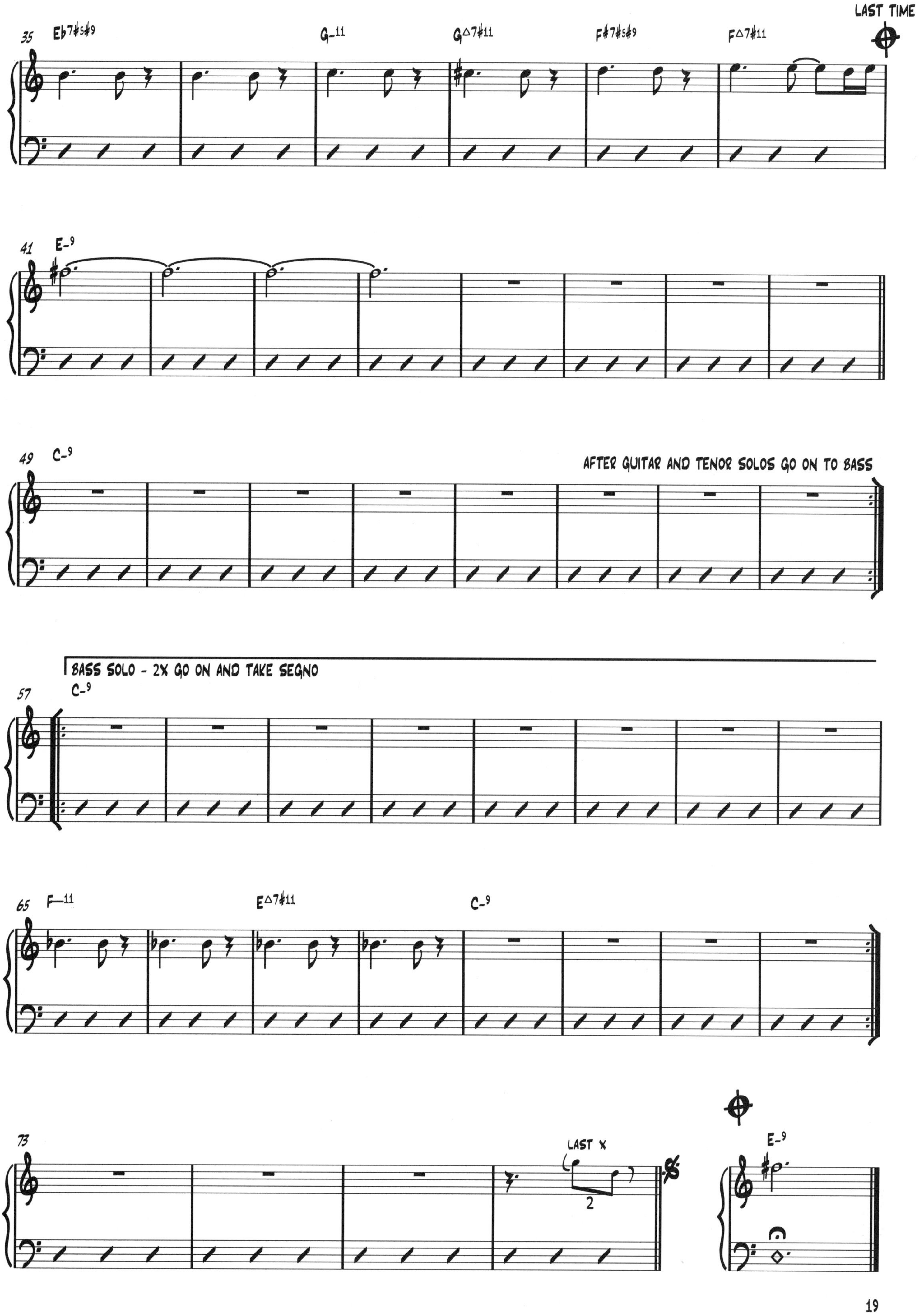
LAST TIME
35
Eb7#5#9
G-11
G△7#11
F#7#5#9
F△7#11
41
E-9
49
C-9
AFTER GUITAR AND TENOR SOLOS GO ON TO BASS
BASS SOLO - 2X GO ON AND TAKE SEGNO
57
C-9
65
F-11
E△7#11
C-9
73
LAST X
2
E-9

Then and Now

By Pat Metheny

C
17 B/F# Dbsus Db F#-7 B-7 E-7 A-7 E/G# A/G
21 D/F# B- A-7 D7 G#-7b5 G△7 A/G D/F# F△7 Bb△7 A7sus A/G
D
E
GUITAR SOLO
25 F#-7 B-7 E-7 A-7 C-7 F-7 Ab-7 C#-7 C/E E△6 C/E E△6
30 F△7b5/E Db/E Bb△7b5/E F#/E C△7/E B/C Eb△7/G D/F# G△7 Db△7
36 Cadd2 F#△7b5 E△7/G# D△7/F# B-9 F#/A# Bb/D D#-9 Ab-7
F
41 Gb/Bb B Gb/Db B/Eb Db/F B/F# Dbsus Db F#-7

G
CHRIS SOLO 2 OR 3X
B-7 E-7 A-7 E/G# A/G D/F# B- A-7 D7 G#-7b5 G△7 A/G D/F# F△7 Bb△7 A7sus A/G F#-7
H
B-7 E-7 A-7 E/G# A/G D/F# B- A-7 D7 G#-7b5 G△7 A/G D/F#
F△7 Bb△7 A7sus A/G F#-7
I
B-7 E-7 A-7 E/G# A/G D/F#
B- A-7 D7 G#-7b5 G△7 A/G D/F# F△7 Bb△7 A7sus A/G
J
F#-7 B-7 E-7 A-7 C-7 F-7 Ab-7 C#-7
K
GUITAR SOLO OUT
C/E E△6 C/E E△6
C/E E△6 C/E E△6 C/E E△6 C/E E△6 C/E E△
RIT.

Breakdealer

By Pat Metheny

B
21 A△7♭5/G♯
25 B♭△7♭5/A
29 D♭△7♭5/C
C
33 G♭maj7(♭5)
Fmaj7(♭5)
E♭maj7(♭5)
Dmaj7(♭5)
D
37 Cmaj7(♭5)
START FIRST SOLO

1ST AND LAST X WITH EXTENSION
41
E
INTERLUDE BETWEEN SOLOS
G/A A/B G/A A/B Bb/C C/D Ebmaj7(b5) Dm11 Gm11 Cm11
45
Gbmaj7(b5) Amaj7(b5) Bmaj7(b5) Dmaj7(b5) Bmaj7(b5) Gbmaj7(b5) G/Db
49
53
FOR SOLOS ON A
LAST TIME

New Year

By Pat Metheny

E7sus4
E9sus4
E7b13 b9
Am13
Cm13
Bbmaj13
A7#9
D9sus4
Cm/D
D7sus4
D
Faster ♩ = 152
G5/D
Cm13/D
A/D
Bbo/D
D5
Eb5/D
D5
Gm/D
E7#9
E7b9
Ebmaj7
F#m7b5
B7
B
Em(add9)
C/E
Em
F#/E
Bmaj7/D#

*Chord symbols reflect overall harmony.

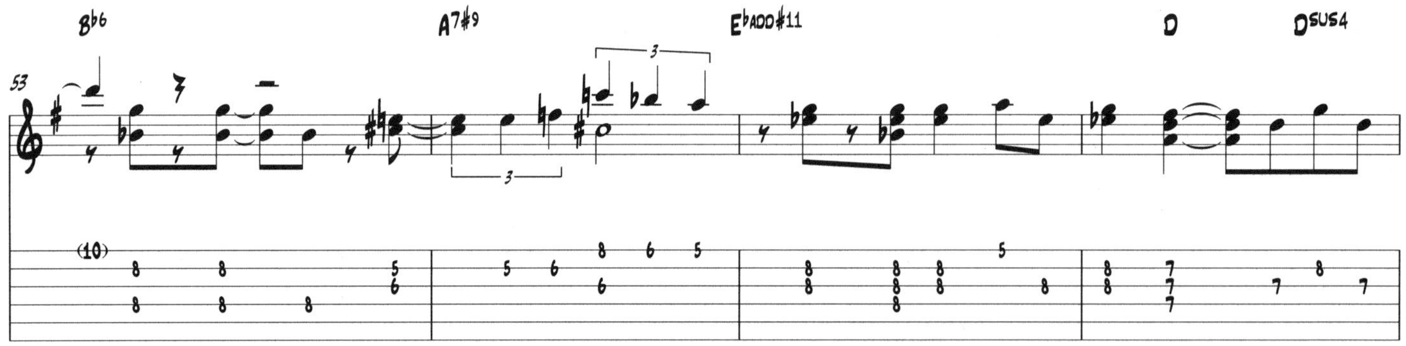

GM/D
CM13/D
A/D
Bbo/D
D
GM
E7
EbMAJ7
A7SUS4
B7
EM11
C
AM9/E
F#/E
BMAJ9/D#
DMAJ13SUS2
GMAJ13
C#M7b5
G/F#
F#
BM
Bb/B
GM9
D5/F
E7#9b9

77
E°
A7b9
F#m11b5
B7
81
E7b9
E9sus4
E7
Am(maj9)
Cm11
85
Bbmaj13
A7b9/C#
Dadd b9
D7b13
89
Gm(maj9)
Cm13/D
A7/D
D7b9
93
Gm(add9)
E7#9 b9
Ebmaj9
B7#9 b9

97
Em(add 4/9)
C/E
E
F#7/E
Badd9/D#
101
Dmaj13
Gmaj9
C#m11b5
Em(add9)
105
Bm(add9)
Gm
Fmaj13
E7b9
109
Em7b13/b5
A7b9
F#m7b5
Bmaj7
113
Fmaj13#11
E7sus4
E7
Am(add9)
Cm7

117
BbMAJ13
A7#9b9/C#
EbMAJ7#11/D
DADD9
121
G/D
GM/D
AM/D
125
GM(ADD9)
CM7
F
BbADD9
EbMAJ7
DMAJ9SUS4
B7b9
D
129
EM
C/E
F#/E
B/D#
133
B5/D
GMAJ9
C#M11b5
F#7b9
BM

137
GM7
C/F
DM/E
E7b9
141
CMAJ7/B
A7 b13 b9
F#M11
B7b13
145
F ADD#11 SUS2
F6/D
E7
AM
CM7
C7SUS 2 4
149
Bb
C/Bb
Bb/C#
A7/C#
C5/D
D7
D7 #9 b9
153
GM7/D
CM/D
A/D
D7

157
Gm(add9)
E7b13#9
E♭maj7sus2
F#m7b5
B7b13
161
Em11
Cmaj7/E
C6/9/E
F#/E
B6/D#
165
D6
Gmaj7
C#m7b5
F#7#9b9
169
Bm(maj13)
Gm(maj7)
Dm7/F
E7#9b9
173
E11#9b5
A7b9
F#m7b5
B7sus4
B7b13

177
FMAJ7
ESUS4
E
AM9
CM
181
BbMAJ7
A7b9/C#
A7b5SUS4/D
D7b9
185
GM9/D
CM/D
A/D
D7
189
GM7
CM7
F13
Bb
Eb
A7
B7b13 b9
E
193
EM(ADD9)
C5/E
F#/E
B/D#

197
D6
Gadd9
C#m11b5
F#7
201
Bm11
Gm
Dm/F
D5/E
E7
205
Em7
A7
F#m7b5
B7#9
209
Fmaj7#11/E
E7sus2/4
E7b9
Am9
Cm7
213
Ab13
Bbo/C#
Ebadd#11/D
Ebo/D

GM/D CM/D A/D D7SUS4 D7
217
GM CM7 F7 B♭MAJ7 E♭MAJ7 A7 AM7♭5 B7♯9
221
F
EM(ADD9) C/E EM F♯/E B/D♯
225
DMAJ9 GMAJ7SUS2 C♯M11♭5 F♯
229
BM9 GM6 DM/F DM/E E7♭9
233

E°
A13b9
F#m7b5
C7
B7
237
Fmaj7
E9sus4
Am
Cm13
241
Bb6
A7 b13 b9/C#
Ebadd#11/D
D
245
Gm/D
Cm13/D
A/D
Bb°/D
D7sus4
D7
249
G
Gm
Cm7
F7sus4
Bb7sus2
Ebmaj7
A7
D7sus4
253

Gm7 Cm7 F13 Bb7sus2 Ebmaj7 A7b13 D7#9b9
257
Gm7 Cm7 F9 Bb7sus4 Eb6/9 A7b13 D7
261
Gm Cm7 F7sus4 Bb6/9 Ebmaj7 A7 D7
265
Gm Cm7 F9 Bb13 Eb9 D7#9b9
269
Gm7 Cm11 F9sus4 F7 Bb13 Bb7b13 Eb6/9 A7b13 A7 D7#9b9
273

GM/Bb Eb CM7 Eb EbADD#11 Bb13 Bb7b13 Eb6/9 A7b13 D7#9/b9
GM7 CM7 F7SUS4 BbSUS2 EbMAJ7 A7 D7SUS4 D7
GM CM7 F Bb7 EbMAJ7 A7 D7SUS4
RIT.
FREE TIME
F#M7b5 B7#9 EM(ADD9) F#11/E

ROOFDOGS

BY PAT METHENY

A7(NO3RD)
CMAJ9
A7(NO3RD)
DSUS4
EM(ADD4)
A7(NO3RD)
CMAJ9
EM(ADD4)
A7(NO3RD)
CMAJ9
EM7
EM(ADD4)
A7(NO3RD)
CMAJ7SUS2
EM11

A7(NO3RD)
CMAJ9
BMAJ13#11 (NO3RD)
A7(NO3RD)
EM(ADD4)/G
FMAJ9
EM(ADD4)
A7(NO3RD)
CMAJ9
EM11
E7#9b9
C
HALF-TIME FEEL
ASUS2/4
AADD9
ASUS2/4
A
AADD9
E5
ASUS2/4
A11
ASUS2/4
AADD9
ASUS2/4
AADD9
E5
FMAJ13#11 (NO3RD)
END HALF-TIME FEEL

D
Em(add4)
A7(no3rd)
Cmaj9
Em11
Em(add4)
A7(no3rd)
Cmaj7sus2
Fmaj7
E
Em
A7(no3rd)
C5
Gtr. synth off
E9sus4
Esus2
A7
C5
Em11

B♭5ADD♯11
C5
A/C♯
C5
C5/B♭
A7
GSUS2
F
G/F
EM7
A
C5
EM11
E7SUS4
A6SUS 2 4
CMAJ13
ESUS4
E5
A7SUS4
CMAJ7SUS2
LET RING
EM11
LET RING
B♭ADD♯11 SUS2
C6SUS2

93
DSUS2
CSUS4
FMAJ13
A
GMAJ7(NO3RD)
DM6/F
E5
A5
97
C
E5
LET RING
F
HALF-TIME FEEL
101
AADD4
AADD9
AADD4
A
W/ GTR. SYNTH (TRUMPET PATCH W/ ECHO)
LET RING
END HALF-TIME FEEL
105
ASUS2
ESUS4
FMAJ7#11(NO3RD)
BM7
G
109
EM(ADD4)
A7
CMAJ13(NO3RD)
EM11

112
A9
115
C13
3
E7sus2
E7sus 2/4
Em(add9)
Fmaj7(no3rd)/E
119
E°/B♭
C13♭9
Dsus4
Cmaj9
B♭maj7(no3rd)
B♭13♯11(no3rd)
Gm(add9)/A
8va
loco
122
Gsus2
Fmaj13
E7sus4
A13♯9
Cmaj13
Em9
126
Em(maj9)
Em11
Em
A7(no3rd)

CMAJ13
EM7
EM(ADD4)
LET RING
LET RING
EM11
ASUS2
A7b9 (NO3RD)
C13SUS2
EM11
A7b9 (NO3RD)
C13 (NO3RD)
GADD9/D
C6SUS 2 4
BbMAJ13#11 (NO3RD)
GM(ADD9)/A
LET RING
GM(ADD9)
EM
A7SUS2
CMAJ13

EM11
LET RING
H
HALF-TIME FEEL
ASUS4 A
ASUS4 AADD9
A13(NO3RD)
ASUS2 4 AADD9
ASUS2 4 A
ASUS4 A9
ASUS2 4 AADD9
ASUS2 4 A
ASUS4
F5ADD#11
FMAJ7(NO3RD)
FMAJ13(NO3RD)
EM(ADD4)
A7(NO3RD)

CMAJ13
EM11
EM(ADD4)
A7 (NO3RD)
CMAJ7SUS2
FMAJ13#11
EM11

Come and See

By Pat Metheny

Gtr. 1: Capo IX

A

Freely ♩ = 115

*42-str. Pikasso gtr. arr. for acous. gtr.
**Symbols in parentheses represent chord names respective to capoed guitar. Symbols above reflect actual sounding chords. Capoed fret is "0" in tab. Chord symbols reflect implied harmony.

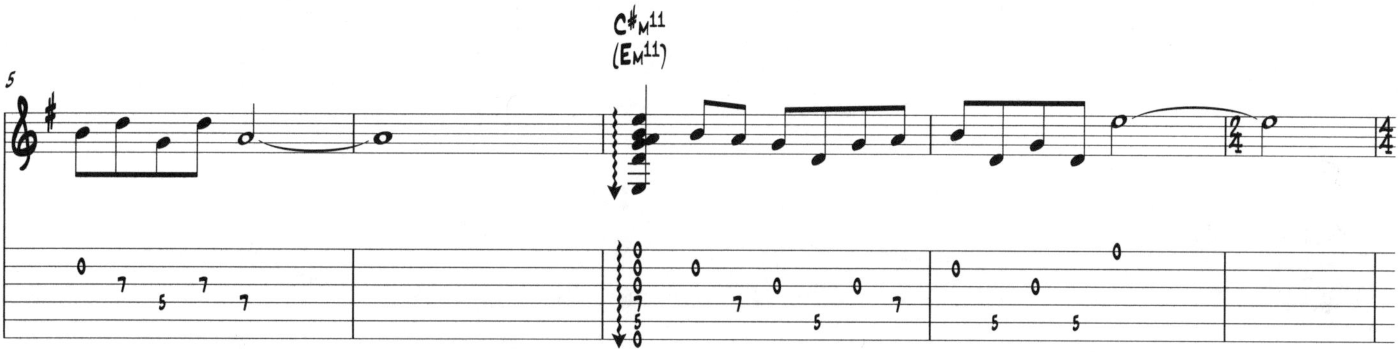

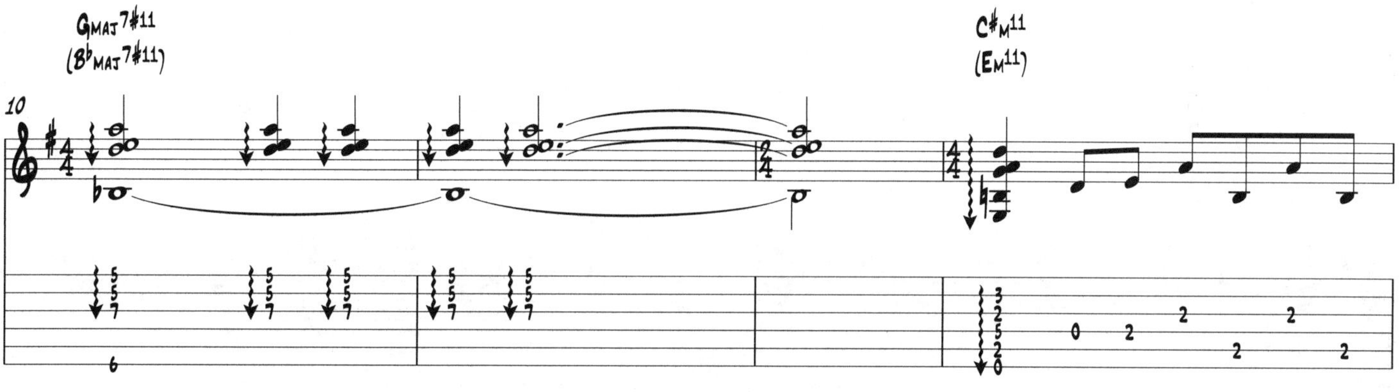

Bm13/F#
(Dm13/A)
C#m11
(Em11)
Gmaj7#11
(B♭maj7#11)
C#m11
(Em11)
w/ finger tips
B
Faster ♩ = 155
C#m11
(Em11)
w/ finger tips
w/ finger tips

Gtr. 1 tacet
Gtr. 2 (elec.)
mf
w/ clean tone
C
*C#m11
*Chord symbols reflect overall harmony.
Asus4
F#sus4
Dsus4
Bsus4
C#5add#11
C#7#11(no3rd)
F6
C#add9
C#7b13sus4
C#m11
Asus4
F#sus4

58
Dsus4
Bsus4
F#9sus4
F#9
62
E13sus4
E13
Dmaj13
E13sus4
67
E13
F#9sus4
F#9
E13sus4
E13
72
Dmaj13
C#m11

D
C#m11
*Played behind the beat where indicated.

94
97
100
F#11
E13sus4
E13#11
104
D6/9 add#11
Dmaj13
E13sus4
108
F#9sus4
F#7
E6/9

DMAJ7#11
DMAJ13#11
C#M11
1/2
*HARM.
*T.H.
*HARM.
*HARM.
*1ST-STR. ONLY.

F#9
F#sus4
F#
Amaj13
Dmaj13#11

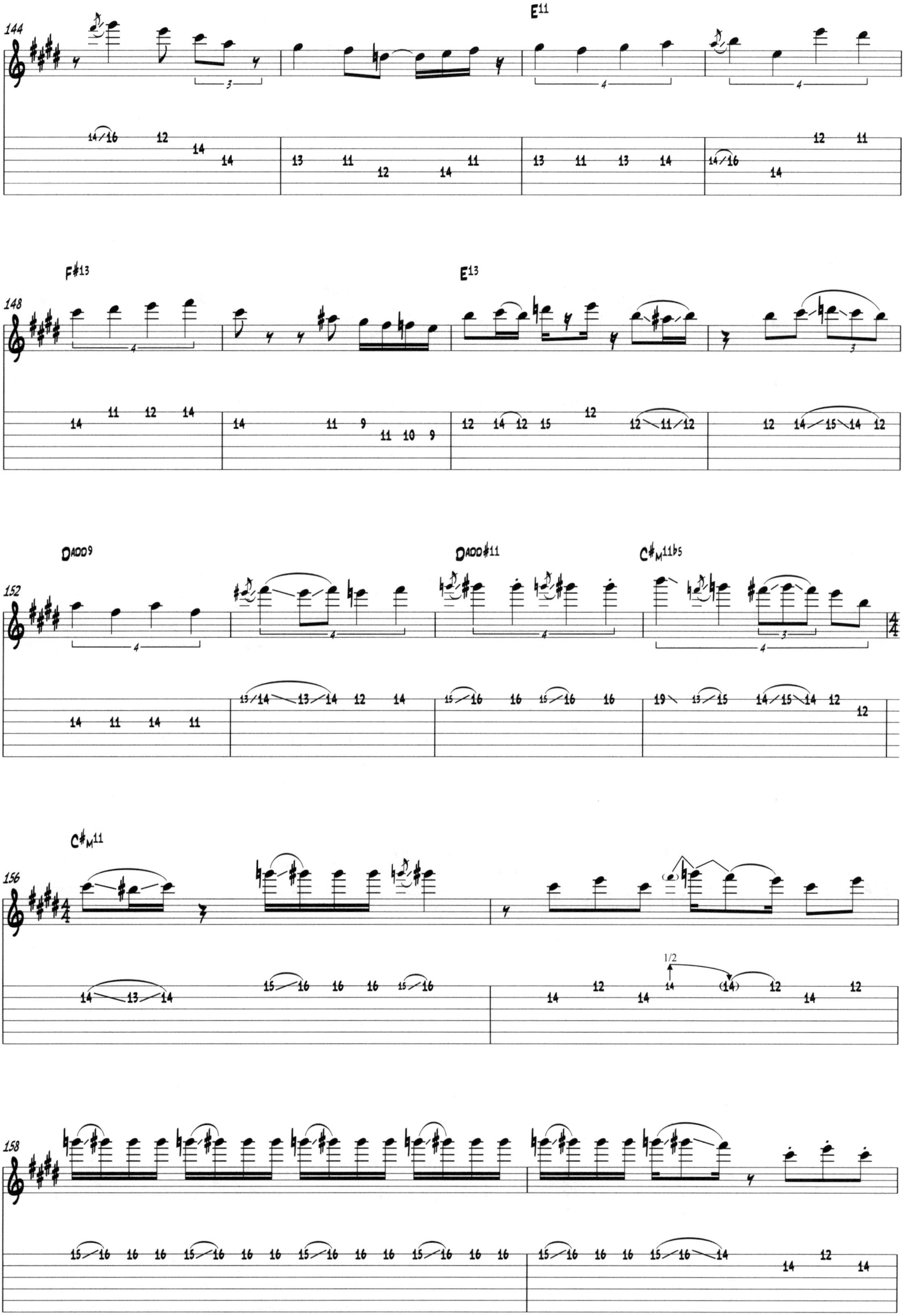
144
E11
148
F#13
E13
152
DADD9
DADD#11
C#M11b5
156
C#M11
158

160
162
E
164
C#5
DMAJ7b9
168
Ab7#9
Eb7#9
E7SUS4
F#7SUS4
C#M7b9
F#7SUS4
172
C#M7
A7
C#M7
C#SUS4
C5
D#7SUS4
C#SUS4
F#
F#M

C#sus4 Gmaj7sus4 G7sus4 D13 C#5
176
F#sus4 F# Asus4 E7 Dmaj13
180
E9sus4 E F#7 F#sus4 F# E7sus4
186
E7 Dmaj13 C#m11
191
196
LET RING

200
204
G#7SUS4 A#7SUS4 C#M11 F#SUS4 ASUS4 Eb5 FSUS4 F#SUS4
208
GSUS4 AbSUS4 ASUS4 GSUS4 AbSUS4 BSUS4 BbSUS4 CSUS4 ASUS4 BbSUS4 DbSUS4 ESUS4
212
BSUS2 G#SUS2 FSUS2 C#M(ADD4) BSUS4 A#SUS4 ASUS4 G#7SUS4 GMAJ7SUS4 F#7SUS4 F7SUS4 E7SUS4
216
Eb7SUS4 F#7SUS4 GMAJ7SUS4 F#7SUS4 D9SUS4 GMAJ11 F#7SUS4 GMAJ7SUS4 A13 G#MAJ7SUS4 AMAJ7SUS4
LET RING

F#11
E7SUS4
E7ADD#11 SUS4
E7SUS4
AMAJ7
AMAJ7SUS4
220
AMAJ7
AMAJ7SUS4
A#7SUS4
E
E11
E
E11
F11
F#11
F
225
F#
F#11
E11
DMAJ7
D6
229
B/D
C#M11
234
238
LET RING

241
AM
LET RING
W/ PICK &
FINGERS
F
244
DM11
248
AM9
Bb MAJ13
252
AM9
GM13
256
FMAJ13#11
G9SUS4

AM(ADD9)
260
DM13
AM(MAJ9)
264
B♭6/9 ADD#11
AM
268
A♭M11
GM11
CADD9/F
272
G9SUS4
G#9SUS4
C#M(ADD9)
276

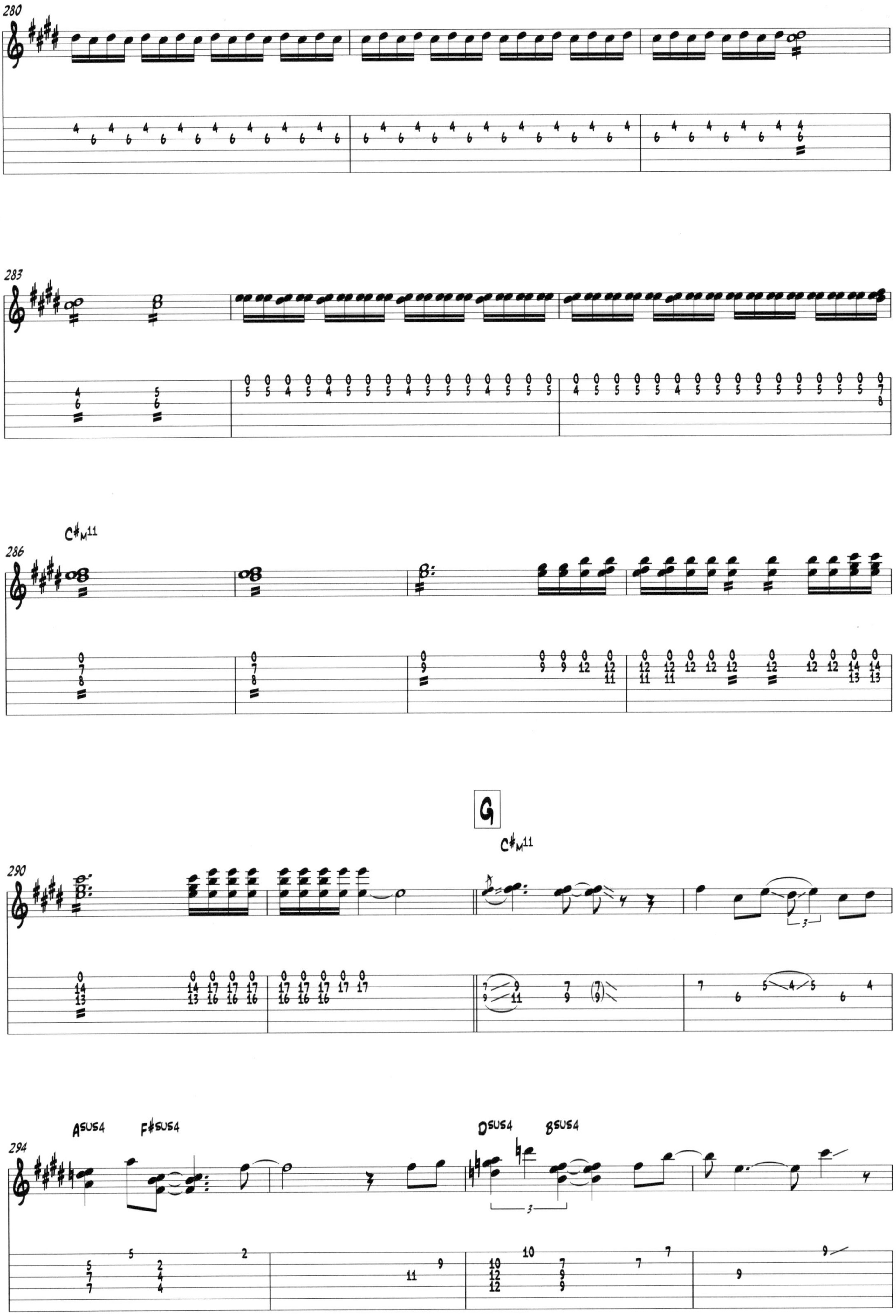
280
283
C#M11
286
G
290
C#M11
Asus4
F#sus4
Dsus4
Bsus4
294

C#M(ADD9)
298
302
ASUS4
F#SUS4
DSUS4
BSUS4
F#9SUS4
F#9
306
E13SUS4
E13
DMAJ13
310
E13SUS4
F#9SUS4
F#9
E13SUS4
314

E13
DMAJ13
C#M11
319
H
C#M11
324
328
C5
332
336

This Belongs to You

By Pat Metheny

F7#11 B♭add♭9 E♭maj9 Dm11♭5 Cmaj9 C#m11 F#add9 B7sus4 B
C
Eadd9/G# Am13 D13sus4 G13♭9 Cmaj7 B7 Em9♭13 Dm13 Cmaj7 Bm11 D11 B♭o7 G/B A(♭5)sus2
G/D B♭7/A♭ E♭maj7/G E♭7/G A♭maj7 A♭m11 Emaj9/G# Bm11 E
A13 Dmaj7(no3rd) Am D13 G5 G6sus2 F#sus4 F#
Bmaj7 Em(add9) A7sus2 D11 G Em(add9) F#m7

D
Bm(add4)
E13sus4
B5
Bm11
Harm.
E13sus2
Em13
Bm(add4)
B5
Fmaj13#11
Gmaj13#11
Bm11
*Played ahead of the beat.
E13sus4
B♭sus4
B7♭13

Em9 E7sus4 Em13 Esus4 Em(add4) Em13 Em11 Bm9
Bm11 Em11/D Fmaj13#11 A9sus4 B♭9sus4 C9sus4 B♭9sus4 A9sus4
*As before
Fmaj13#11sus2 Gmaj7#11
Cmaj7#11 D/A E/G D/F# Cmaj7
E
A tempo
Fmaj7#11 Esus2 Am13 A7sus4 Dm13 G13♭9 Cmaj7 B7♭13
rit.

*Tremolo pick w/ tip of finger.

Leaving Town

By Pat Metheny

A7#9b9/C#
Dm
DbADD9
AbADD9
C9SUS4
FADD9
DbADD9
AbADD9
EbADD9
BbADD9
CSUS4
CADD9
DbMAJ9#11
BbM7
CSUS4
C
DbMAJ9#11
BbM9
Eb9SUS4
AbMAJ7
C#SUS2 4
DADD#11
G#M/A
E11
AADD9
DM(MAJ9)
G11
BADD#9
BADDb9
F
AM
EbADD9 #11
D13SUS4
D
D9SUS4
D

D9sus4
Gmaj9
Fmaj9
Bm7
F6/9
B7b13/D#
Dm7
C
Gadd9/B
Am9
G5
B
G7
G7
1/2
1/4

*Played behind the beat.
E♭maj13#11

G7
*As before

Emaj13#11
95
99
102
105
108
8va
LOCO
C7

Am7
D/A
Cmaj7
D/C
G/A
C/A
Bm
Cmaj13#11 (no3rd)
Asus2
Cmaj7
D9sus4
C
Gmaj7
Fmaj9
Gadd9/B
Fmaj9
B9b13/D#
Dm13
*Harm.
Harm.
*Top note only.

D
133
G5
Fsus2
G5
137
Fsus2
G5
Fsus2
G6sus2
141
G9sus4
G
F
G
146
F
G
Fsus2
Gsus2
F
G5
E♭maj7
151
Dm7
E♭maj7
D sus4 add♭9
E♭maj7
Dm7
E♭maj7

156
Dm11 G5 Dm Ebmaj7sus2
160
Dm7 Ebmaj7 Bbmaj7sus2 Dm7 Ebmaj7 Dm11 Ebmaj7
164
Dm11 Ebmaj13 Dm11 Gsus2
168
F5 F#5/F Gsus2 Ebmaj7#11(no3rd)/D Dsus4 Fsus2 Dbmaj7#11(no3rd)/G Eb5/D F#maj7sus4/G
172
F#7sus4/C A5/F Ebsus2/G Emaj7sus4/C# Fmaj13 G5add b13 G5

176 Fsus2 G5 F7sus4 G5 Fsus2 G5 Fsus2 G5
181 Fsus2 G5 Amaj7sus4 B♭maj7sus4 Dm7 E♭maj7
185 Dm7 E♭5 Dm7 E♭5 Dm7 E♭5
189 Dm7 Dmaj7 E5/D Dmaj7 Dm7/E♭ Dmaj7/E♭ E5/E♭ Dm7 Dmaj7/E♭
193 E5/E♭ Dmaj7/E♭ Dm7/E♭ Dmaj7 E5/D Dmaj7 E5/D Dm7

197
Dmaj7 Dm7 Dmaj7 Dm7 C B♭5add♯11 C
201
B♭5add♯11 C B♭5add♯11 C B♭5add♯11 C
205
C11 C/B♭ C Am9 Bm7 Cmaj7
209
Bm7 Em/A Bm7 Cmaj7 Am9 Cmaj7
214
G5 F5 G5 Em/G Dm7 G5

219
Dm7 G5 F5 G5 G9sus4 G/C
E
224
F5/Bb C/E Am/Bb E9b13/G# Gm7 D7/F# F Cadd9/E Dm7
229
G13 Csus4 Cmaj7 Fmaj7 Gm9 D/F# Fm13 Ebmaj11
233
Abm(add4) Db9sus4 Gbmaj7 C9sus4 Fmaj9 Ebmaj9 F/A
237
Ebmaj7 A7b13/C# Dm7b13 Gm9 C13 (no3rd) F13 G5/B

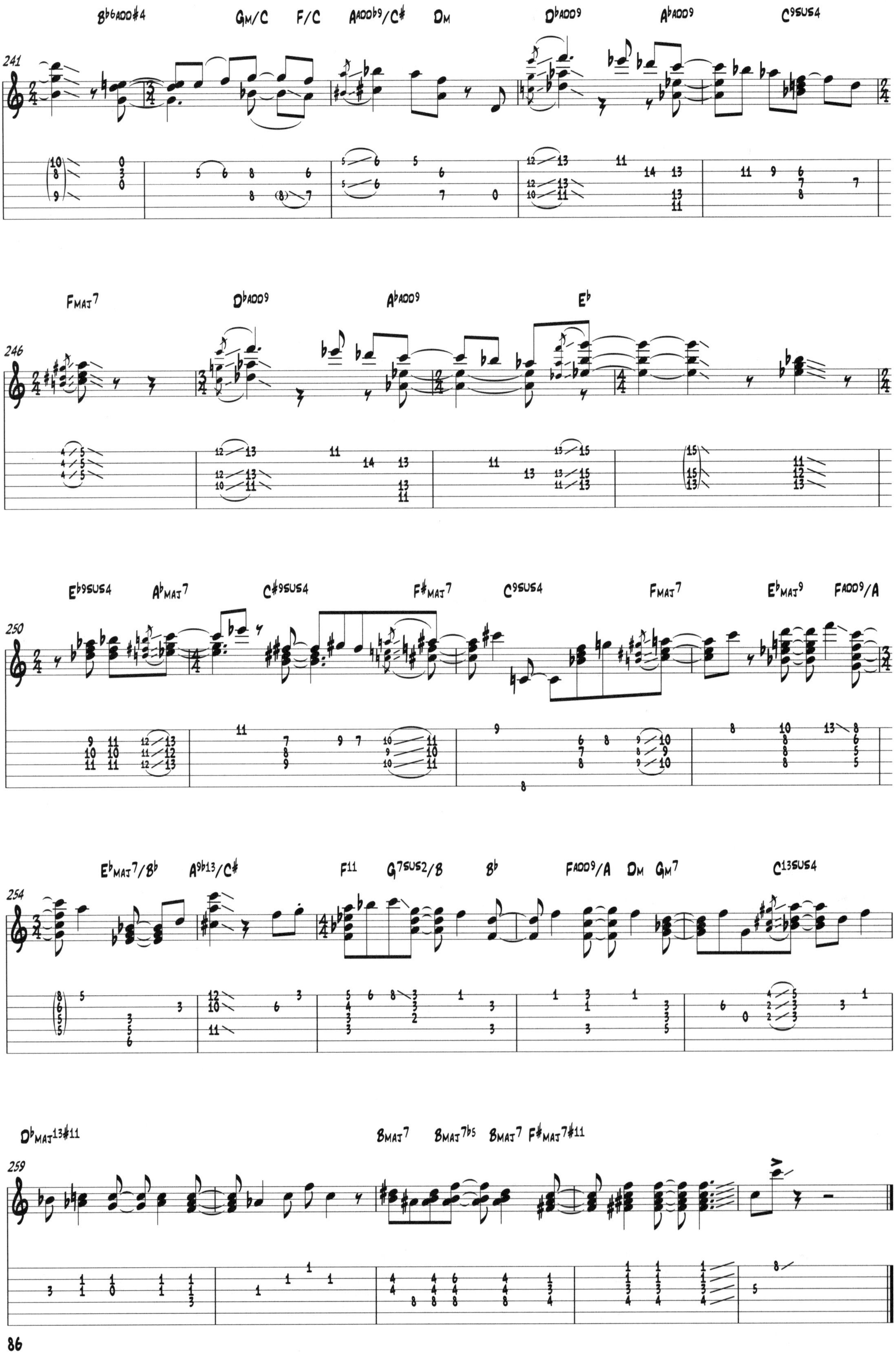
Bb6add#4 Gm/C F/C Aaddb9/C# Dm Dbadd9 Abadd9 C9sus4
241
Fmaj7 Dbadd9 Abadd9 Eb
246
Eb9sus4 Abmaj7 C#9sus4 F#maj7 C9sus4 Fmaj7 Ebmaj9 Fadd9/A
250
Ebmaj7/Bb A9b13/C# F11 G7sus2/B Bb Fadd9/A Dm Gm7 C13sus4
254
Dbmaj13#11 Bmaj7 Bmaj7b5 Bmaj7 F#maj7#11
259

Interval Waltz

By Pat Metheny

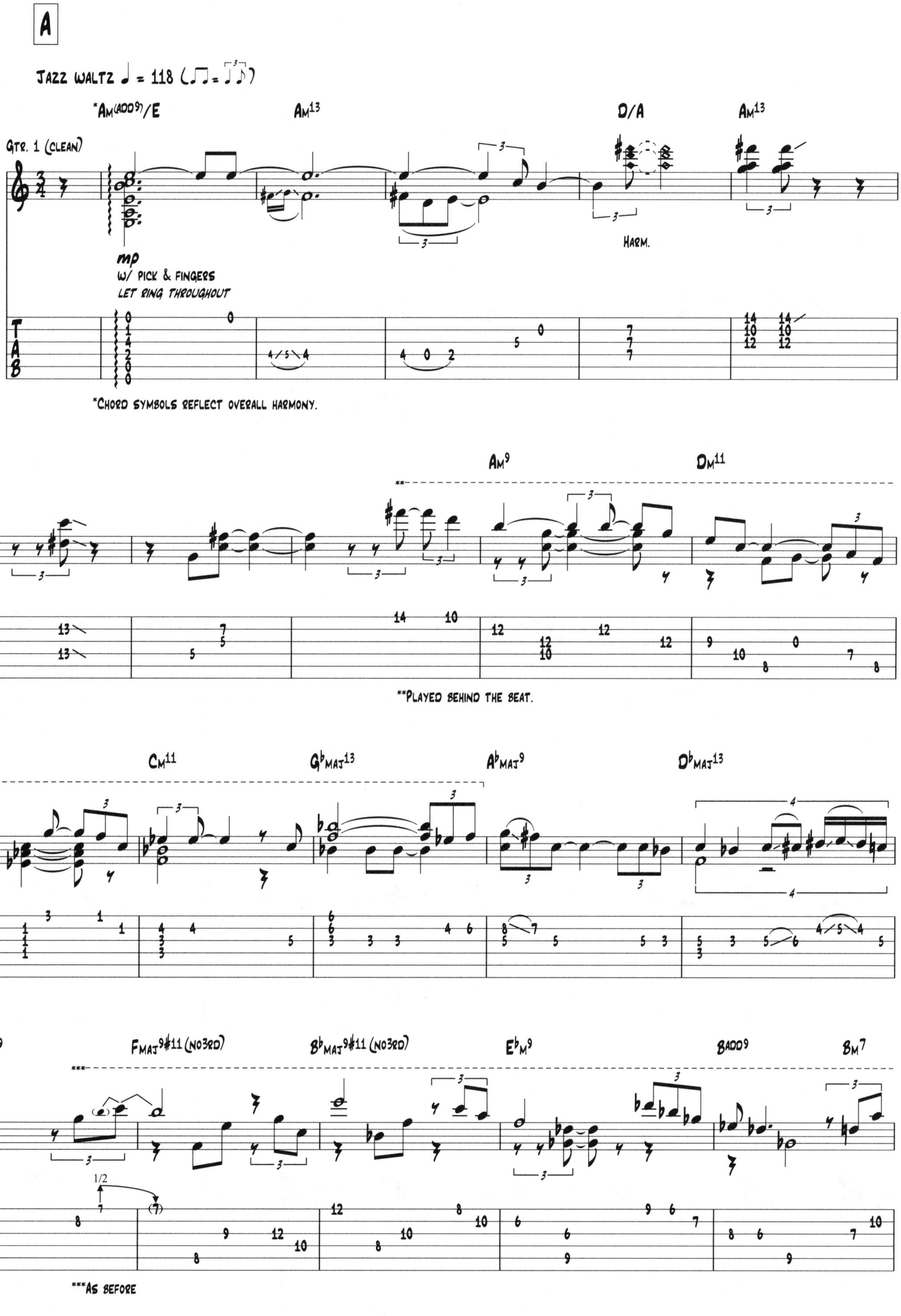

Em9
Fadd#11/A
E♭maj7#11/G
Dmaj13
Dsus2
Dmaj7#11(no3rd)
Dmaj13
Dmaj7#11
Dmaj13
Dmaj7#11(no3rd)
Fm9
Fm11
Emaj13
Am11
D#7♭13 #9
Gm9/D
F#m11
F#add#9
Fmaj13#11

8
EM(ADD 2/4)
EM
8VA
LOCO
CM
AM(MAJ11)
DM9
FM
CM7
*AS BEFORE

GbMAJ9 (NO3RD)
Ab6ADD#11
DbMAJ7#11
A7#9b9
FMAJ13b9
BbMAJ13#11
Eb13
BM(MAJ11)
BM9
*As before.
EM(ADD4)
ASUS4
GSUS2
GM
8VA
DADD9
8VA
LOCO
STEADY GLISS.
DMAJ7#5
D13/A
DMAJ13
D6/9 ADD#11
**As before

D♭/F G m/F A♭/F
B♭/F Cm/F Fm
E F#/E Emaj7
F#6/E
Am13
Cm/E♭ F#m7/E♭ Gmaj7/E♭
E♭maj13 (no3rd)
E♭/G Gm11
F#m7
Dadd9/F#
Fmaj9#11
Em13
Em11♭5
1/2
1/2

*As before

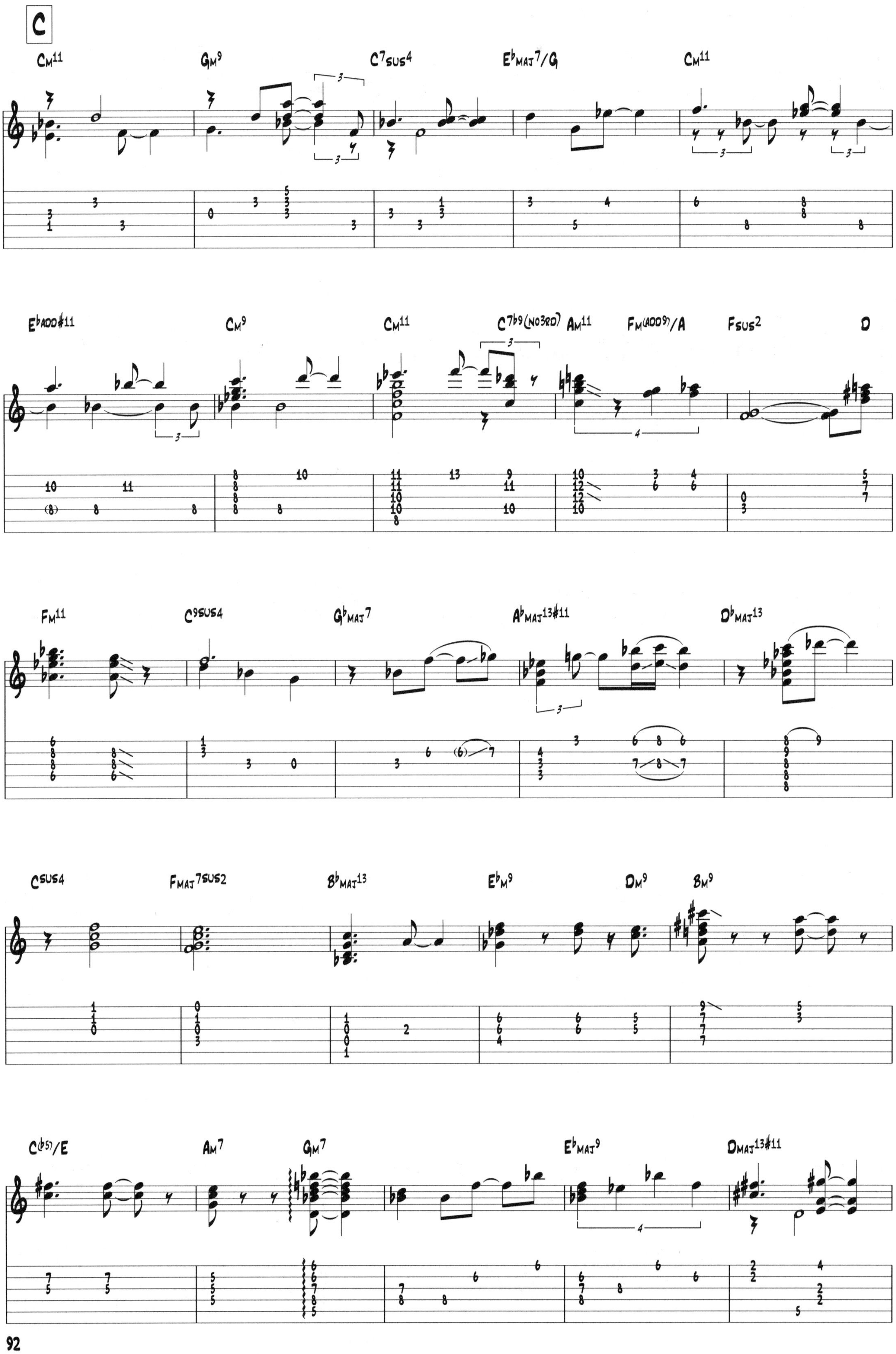
C
Cm11 Gm9 C7sus4 Ebmaj7/G Cm11
Ebadd#11 Cm9 Cm11 C7b9(no3rd) Am11 Fm(add9)/A Fsus2 D
Fm11 C9sus4 Gbmaj7 Abmaj13#11 Dbmaj13
Csus4 Fmaj7sus2 Bbmaj13 Ebm9 Dm9 Bm9
C(b5)/E Am7 Gm7 Ebmaj9 Dmaj13#11

Fm11
E6/9 add#11
Am9
D/A
Eb7 b13 #9
Gm11
Gadd#11
F#7 b13 #9
Fmaj7#11(no3rd)
Em9
Bm7
Harm.
Em9
A5/B
B5/A

E9sus4
G/B
A5/B
Cm11
G9sus4
Cm13
C9sus4
Dm/C
Gm(add9)
Cm11
D
Cm9
Cm11
Fm9
Bmaj7
Bmaj13
C6sus2

F5
F7sus2
Gm
Emaj7(no3rd)
E7(no3rd)
Cm9
Fm9
Bmaj13
Cm9
tr
Cm11
P.M.
E
Am9
Dm7
Fm9
*As before

Cm
G♭maj13#11 (no3rd)
A♭maj9
D♭maj13#11 (no3rd)
A7#9
F6/9 add#11
B♭maj13#11
E♭m9
Badd9
Bm7
Em9
Am(add9)
E♭add#11
E♭/G
Dmaj13#11
Fm9

*Bounce pick-hand index or middle finger on 6th str., over the pickups, in indicated rhythm.

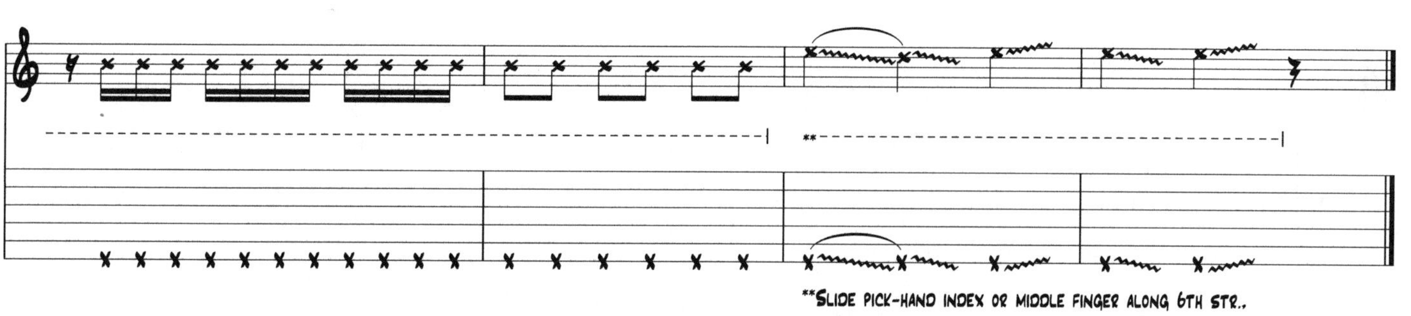

**Slide pick-hand index or middle finger along 6th str., over the pickups, in indicated rhythm and direction.

Signals
(Orchestration Sketch)
By Pat Metheny

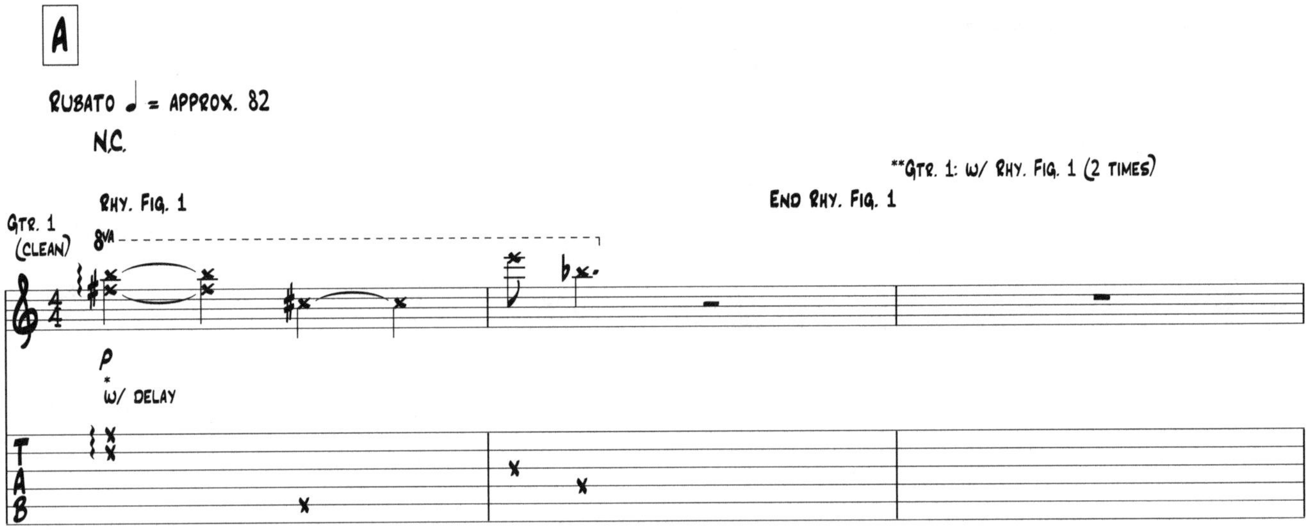

*Pluck strings behind bridge (x's represent approximate pitch).

**Recalled Riffs & Rhy. Figs. are echo repeats (loops) held for the specified duration.

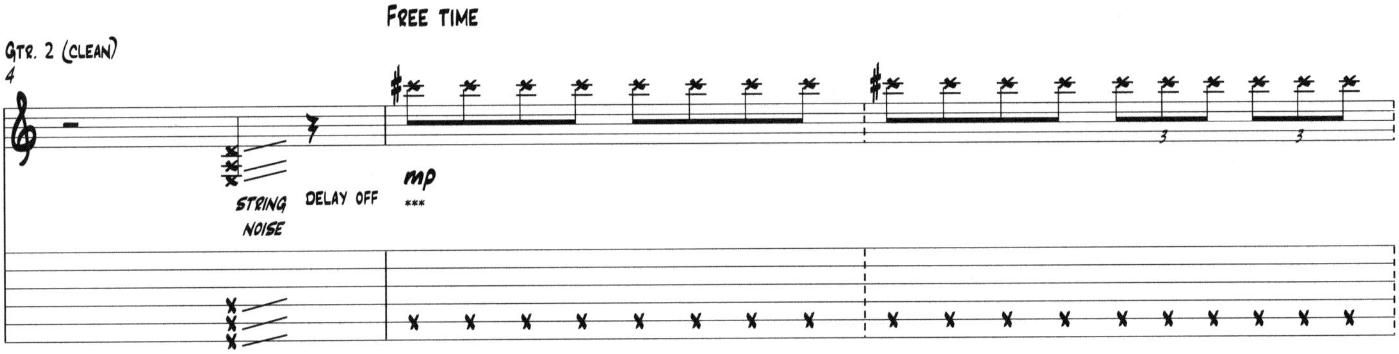

***As before

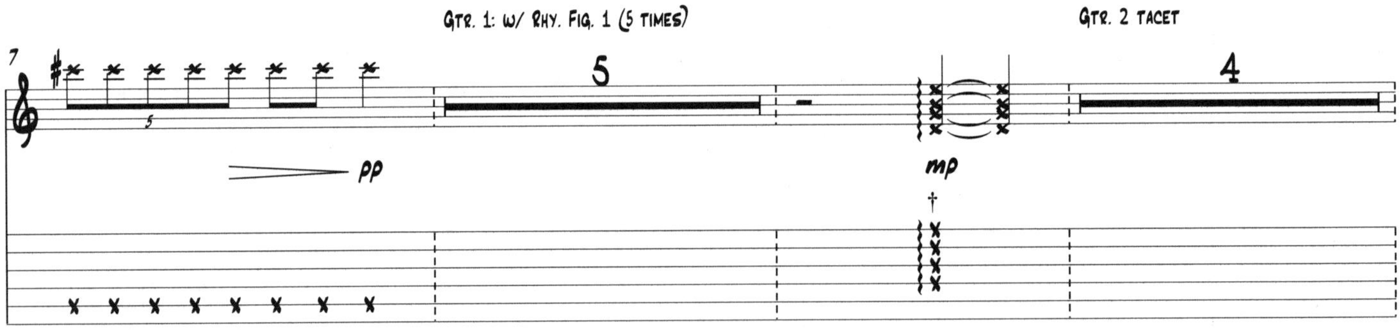

†As before

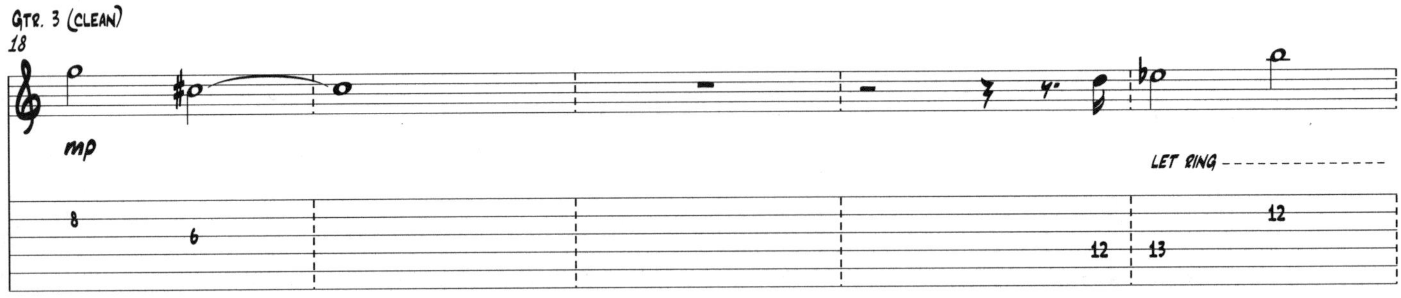

LET RING
LET RING
Gtr. 1: w/ Rhy. Fig. 1 (2 times)
LET RING
LET RING

Very fast ♩ = 180
Gtr. 3 tacet
(Tambourine)
B
G♭maj7#11
Rhy. Fig. 2
End Rhy. Fig. 2
Gtr. 4: w/ Rhy. Fig. 2 (29 times)
Gtr. 4 (clean)
mp

Gtr. 4: w/ Rhy. Fig. 3 (27 times)
Rhy. Fig. 3
End Rhy. Fig. 3
68
p
Gtr. 4: w/ Rhy. Fig. 4 (25 times)
Rhy. Fig. 4
End Rhy. Fig. 4
72
Rhy. Fig. 5
End Rhy. Fig. 5
76
Gtr. 4: w/ Rhy. Fig. 5 (11 times)
80
4
88
4
Riff A
End Riff A

Gtr. 4: w/ Riff A (7 times)
Riff B
End Riff B
Gtr. 4: w/ Riff B (6 times)
Riff C
End Riff C
Gtr. 4: w/ Riff C (5 times)
Riff D
End Riff D
Gtr. 4: w/ Riff D (4 times)

116
120
C
Sax Solo
G♭maj7♯11
Riff E
124
End Riff E
Gtr. 4: w/ Riff E (7 times)
128
28
D
Gtr. 4: w/ Rhy. Fig. 6 (16 times)
Amaj7♯11
Rhy. Fig. 6
End Rhy. Fig. 6
Gtr. 4
156
Riff F
160
End Riff F

Gtr. 4: w/ Riff F (6 1/2 times)
Riff G
End Riff G
Gtr. 4: w/ Riff 6 (12 times)
164
Gtr. 5 (clean)
168
Riff H1
mp
Gtr. 4
Riff H
171
End Riff H1
End Riff H
Gtrs. 4 & 5: w/ Riffs H & H1 (4 times)
Riff I
Gtr. 4
174
End Riff I

Gtr. 4: w/ Riff I (3 times)
Riff J
End Riff J
178
(6)
Gtr. 4: w/ Riff J (2 times)
Riff K
End Riff K
182
Gtr. 4: w/ Riff K
186
E
Sax Solo
Amaj7#11
Riff L1
End Riff L1
Gtr. 6 (clean)
190
mp
Gtr. 4
Riff L
End Riff L

F
Guitar Synth Solo
Gtrs. 4 & 6: w/ Riffs L & L1 (9 times)
*Gtr. 7 (gtr. synth)
Amaj7#11
35
mf
*Set for one octave above.

253
258
262
266
G♭MAJ7♯11
270

274
Amaj7#11
278
282
G♭maj7#11
286
290

Amaj7#11
294
8va
298
8va
301
8va
305
8va
D♭
D♭/C
B♭m7
D♭/F
310
8va
LOCO

*Played behind the beat.

D♭
D♭/C
B♭m7
D♭/F
334
G♭maj7
338
8va
Amaj7
LOCO
342
8va
D♭
D♭/C
B♭m7
D♭/F
346
8va
G♭maj7
LOCO
350

G

Outro

Gtr. 4: w/ Rhy. Fig. 6 (12 times)
Gtr. 4: w/ Riff G (12 times)
Gtr. 4: w/ Riff H (6 times)
Gtr. 7 tacet

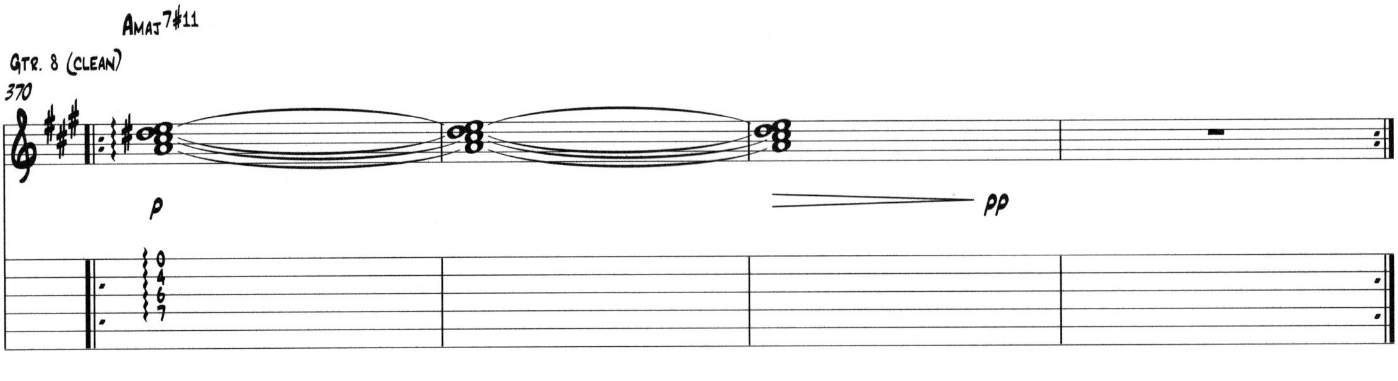

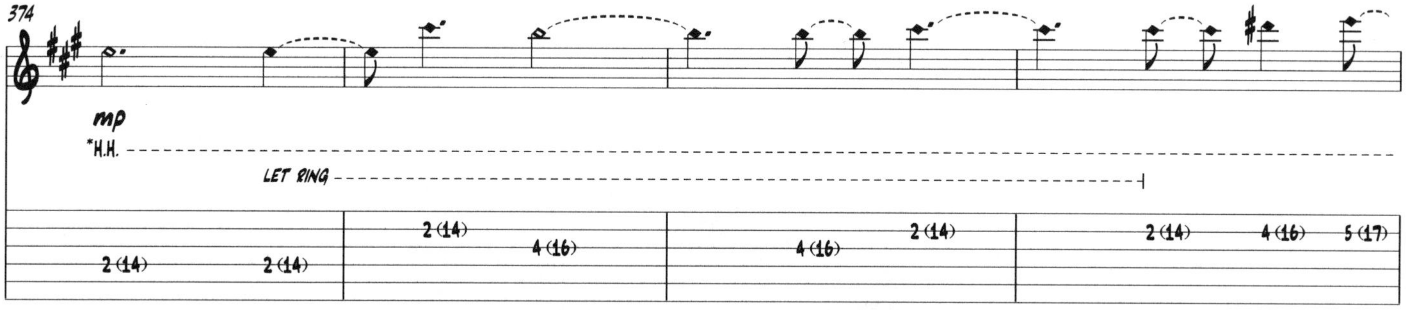

*Harp harmonics produced by lightly touching string 12 frets above fretted note while picking string.

394
*pp < p
1/2
*Vol. Swell
398
mp
P.M.
Let Ring
8va
Let Ring
402
8va
Let Ring
406
8va
pp
Let Ring
410
Loco
p
Let Ring

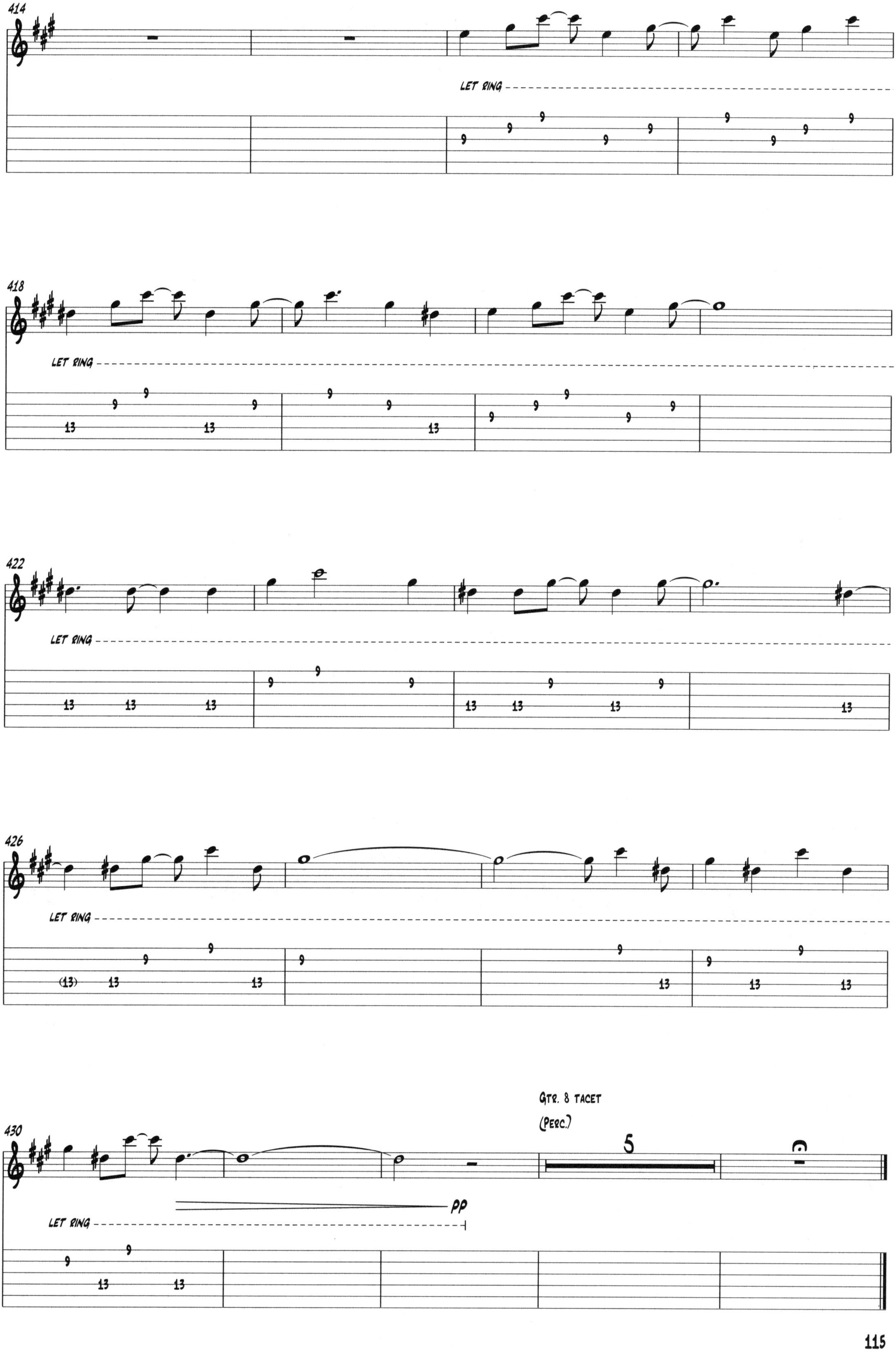
414
LET RING
418
LET RING
422
LET RING
426
LET RING
430
GTR. 8 TACET
(PERC.)
PP
LET RING

THEN AND NOW

BY PAT METHENY

*CHORD SYMBOLS REFLECT IMPLIED HARMONY.

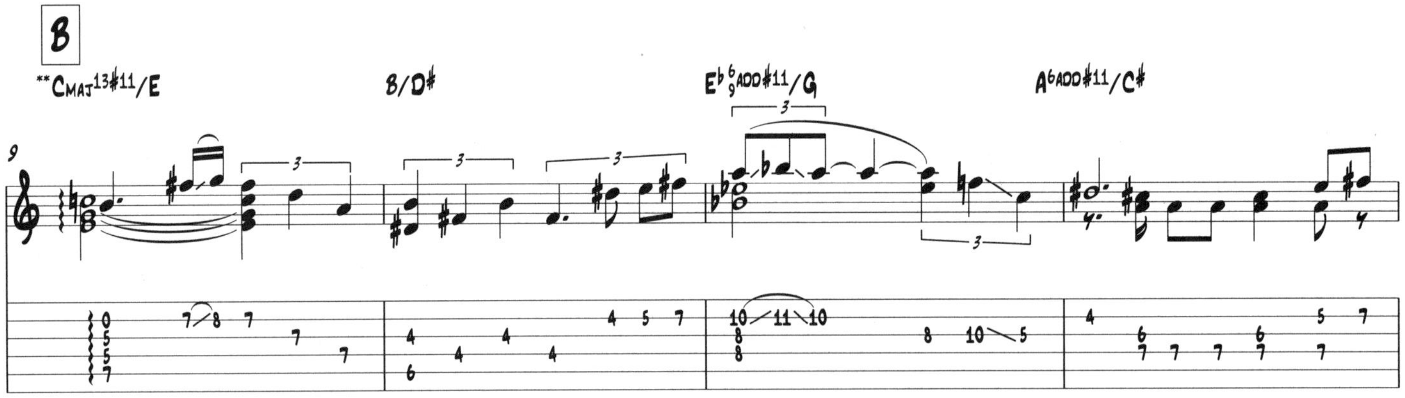

**CHORD SYMBOLS REFLECT OVERALL HARMONY.

CMAJ13(NO3RD)
GbMAJ7#11(NO3RD)
B6/9
EMAJ13#11/G#
DADD#11/9/F#
BM(MAJ9)
BM9
GbSUS2/Bb
D°7
EbM
C
EbM(ADD4)
Db
AbM(ADD9)
GbSUS2/Bb
BADD9
GbMAJ7/Db
B/D#
FM7
BMAJ7/F#
C#9SUS4
C#

D
F#m11 Bm11 Em9 Am9 Esus2/G# A/G
D/F# Bm7 Bbm7 Am7 D9 G#m7b5 Gmaj7 A/G
Dadd9/F# Fmaj13 Bbmaj7#11 Asus2 A13/G
F#m11 Bm11 Em9 Am9 Cm9 Fm9
E
Abm9 Dbm9 Cmaj7#11/E Emaj7sus2 Cmaj7/E Emaj9

F6add#11/E
Db7#9/E
BbMAJ7#11/E
*Played behind the beat.
F#7#9/E
CMAJ7/E
C7#9 Bb7#9 A7#9
B/C
CMAJ#11
Ebadd#11/G
D7b9/F#
D
F#°7
GMAJ7
Bm(add9)
Eb7/Db
DbMAJ7
C7b9
F#add#11
Ab/Db G/A
F#/G#
DMAJ13#11
Bm11
Bb°7 Bb7b13 Em9 Ebm11
**Played behind the beat.

E♭M13
A♭M9
G♭MAJ9/B♭
BADD♯11
D♭6
A♭M9/E♭
D♭/F
C♭MAJ9/G♭
D♭13SUS4
D♭13
F
F♯M7
BM
EM7
AM11
E/G♯
A/G
D/F♯

94
Bm9
B♭m7
Am7
D9
G♯m7♭5
Gmaj7
A/G
98
D/F♯
Fmaj9♯11
B♭maj7
G/A
A/G
102
F♯m7
Bm7
Em7
Am11
E/G♯
A/G
106
D/F♯
E♭/A
Bm7
B♭m7
Am7
D13
G♯m7♭5
Gmaj7
A/G
110
Dadd9/F♯
Fmaj13
B♭maj7sus2/A
A9sus4
A
A9sus4
A

G
F#m11 Bm11 Em9 Am9 Esus2/F# Aadd9/G
*Played behind the beat.
D/F# Bm B♭m7 Am7 D9 G#m7♭9 G5 Aadd9/G
Dadd9/F# Fadd9 B♭maj9#11 G6/A A
F#m7 Bm11 Em9 Am9 E/G# A7/G D/F# Bm7
Am9 D13 G#m7 Gmaj7 A/G

Dsus2/F#
Fmaj7
B♭maj7
A9sus4
134
F#m11
Bm11
Em9
Am9
Cm9
Fm7
A♭m9
D♭m9
138
H
Cmaj7#11/E
Emaj7sus2
Cmaj9#11/E
Esus2
Em
143
*Played behind the beat.
A/E
B♭add#11/E
Aadd9/E
Amaj7sus2/E
148
Cmaj7/E
Cmaj7#11/E
Csus2/E
Cmaj7/E
Esus2
153
rit.

Breakdealer

By Pat Metheny

8
B♭M7♭9
BM9
LET RING
LET RING
LET RING
D
DSUS4
D
DM
DM11
LET RING
D♯M7♭9
E7♯11/G♯
LET RING
AADD♯11
AMAJ9
A6/9 ADD♯11
LET RING
LET RING

AM7b5
37
LET RING
CM7b9
41
LET RING
Gb MAJ 7#11 (NO3RD)
FMAJ 7#11 (NO3RD)
Eb MAJ 9#11 (NO3RD)
DMAJ 9#11 (NO3RD)
45
C
CMAJ 7#11
49
53

BM7b9
BM7b9
DM7b9
DM
EbM7b9

G#M7b9
AM7b9
FM(ADD9)/C
8VA
C7ALT
8VA
LOCO
GbMAJ9#11

FMAJ7
E♭MAJ13
DMAJ7#11
C#MAJ7#11
8VA
LOCO
B♭M7♭9
BM7♭9

DM7b9
D#M7b9
*Played behind the beat.
G#M7b9
Bb/A
Gm(add9)/A
A+sus4
Bbmaj7#11(no3rd)/A
Asus4
F5/A
Bbmaj13/A

D♭add9/C
E♭add9/C
D♭maj7/C
E♭7/C
A♭5/C
B♭5/C
C5
D♭5/C
Cm7
G♭maj7♯11
Fmaj9♯11
E♭maj13
Dmaj13♯11
Cmaj13♯11

135
139
A9sus4 B9sus4
A9sus4 B9sus4 C9sus4
D9sus4 Dm/E♭
143
Dm11
Gm11
Cm9
E♭9sus4/G♭ G♭9sus4/B♭ A♭9sus4/B G♭9sus4/B E♭9sus4/B G♭add 9 #11
D
Gmaj13#11/C#
147
LET RING
152
LET RING
Bm7♭9

156
BM(MAJ9)
LET RING
LET RING
BM7
161
D
DM(ADD9)
LET RING
166
EM11
BSUS2
LET RING
170
G#M7b9
LET RING
174
AM7b9

178
Cm7b9
182
Gmaj7#11
Fmaj7#11
Ebmaj13#11
LET RING
LET RING
LET RING
186
Dmaj13
Cmaj9#11
LET RING
LET RING
190
Bbm7b9
194
Bm(maj7)
Bm7
LET RING

198
Dm7b9
C#/D Dsus4
203
Ebsus4
Esadd#11
Emaj13
207
G#m7b9
211
Am7b9
Cm7b9
216
Gbmaj7#11
Fmaj7#11
LET RING
LET RING

E♭add#11
Dmaj7#11
Cmaj13#11
221
LET RING
LET RING
226
G/A A/B
G/A A/B
B♭/C C/D F6/E♭
Dm11 Gm9
Cm9
230
E♭♭9sus4/G♭ G♭9sus4/B♭ A♭9sus4/B G♭9sus4/D E♭♭9sus4/B
F#sus2
Gmaj13#11/C#
235
LET RING
239

E
Dm7b9
244
249
254
LET RING
LET RING
259
263

267
LET RING
271
275
279
283
F
DM11
B♭M7♭9

287
Bm(maj11)
LET RING
291
Bm11
D
Dsus4
D
LET RING
295
Dm(add4)
E♭m11
LET RING
299
B11/G
G#5addb9
B11/A
LET RING
303
Amaj7sus2
A6/9add#11
Am7b9

CM7b9
LET RING
GbMAJ7#11
FMAJ7#11
EbMAJ7#11
DMAJ7#11
CMAJ13#11
F#M7
B(NO3RD)

GUITAR NOTATION LEGEND

Guitar music can be notated three different ways: on a *musical staff*, in *tablature*, and in *rhythm slashes*.

RHYTHM SLASHES are written above the staff. Strum chords in the rhythm indicated. Use the chord diagrams found at the top of the first page of the transcription for the appropriate chord voicings. Round noteheads indicate single notes.

THE MUSICAL STAFF shows pitches and rhythms and is divided by bar lines into measures. Pitches are named after the first seven letters of the alphabet.

TABLATURE graphically represents the guitar fingerboard. Each horizontal line represents a string, and each number represents a fret.

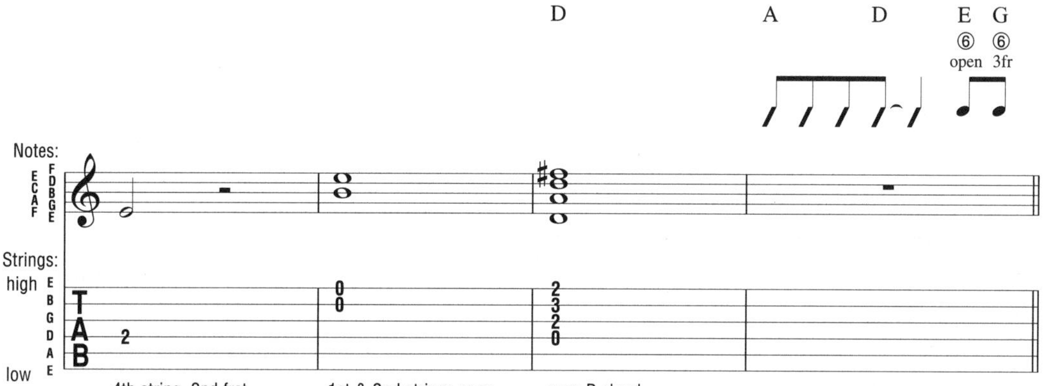

4th string, 2nd fret

1st & 2nd strings open, played together

open D chord

HALF-STEP BEND: Strike the note and bend up 1/2 step.

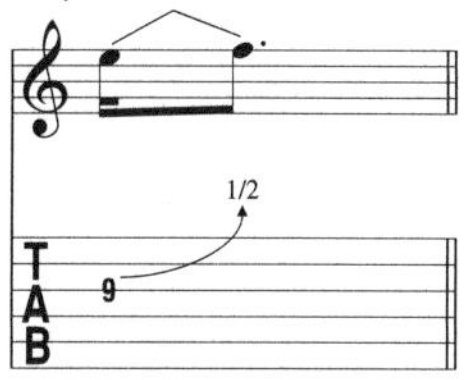

WHOLE-STEP BEND: Strike the note and bend up one step.

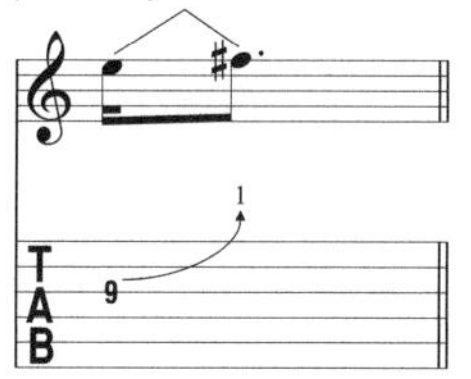

GRACE NOTE BEND: Strike the note and immediately bend up as indicated.

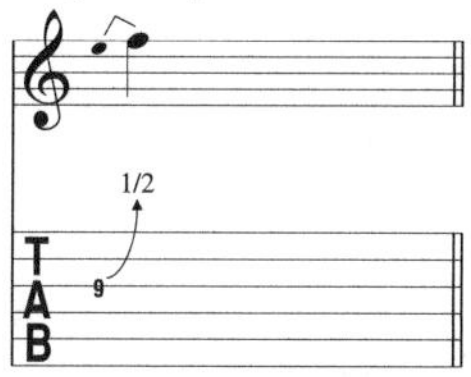

SLIGHT (MICROTONE) BEND: Strike the note and bend up 1/4 step.

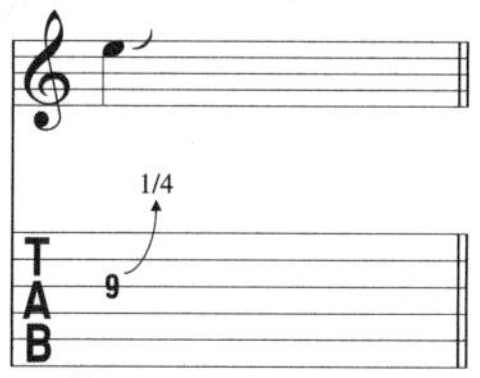

BEND AND RELEASE: Strike the note and bend up as indicated, then release back to the original note. Only the first note is struck.

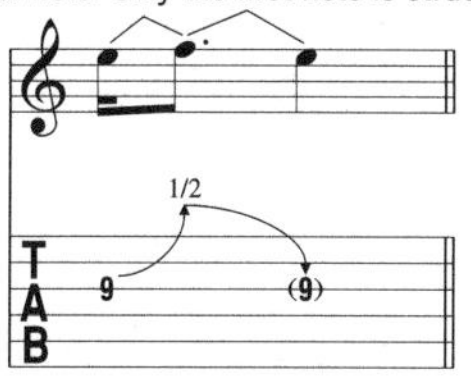

PRE-BEND: Bend the note as indicated, then strike it.

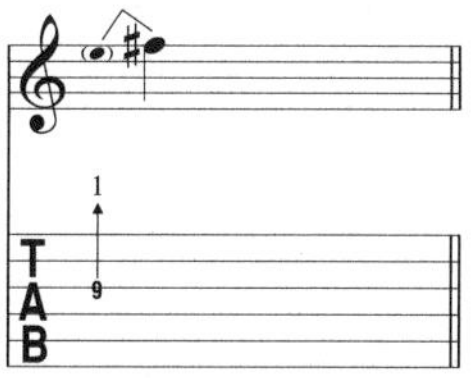

VIBRATO: The string is vibrated by rapidly bending and releasing the note with the fretting hand.

WIDE VIBRATO: The pitch is varied to a greater degree by vibrating with the fretting hand.

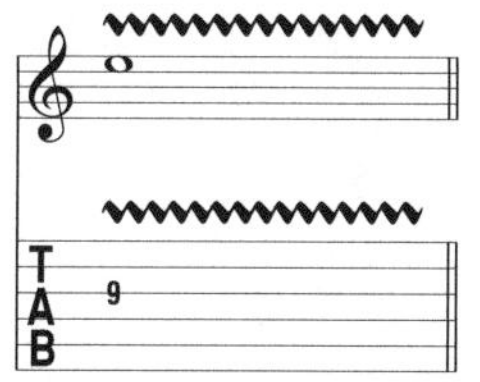

HAMMER-ON: Strike the first (lower) note with one finger, then sound the higher note (on the same string) with another finger by fretting it without picking.

PULL-OFF: Place both fingers on the notes to be sounded. Strike the first note and without picking, pull the finger off to sound the second (lower) note.

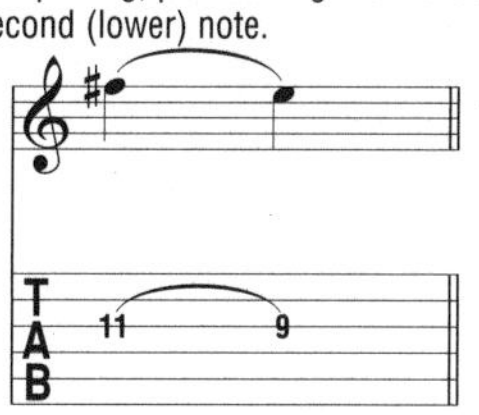

LEGATO SLIDE: Strike the first note and then slide the same fret-hand finger up or down to the second note. The second note is not struck.

SHIFT SLIDE: Same as legato slide, except the second note is struck.

TRILL: Very rapidly alternate between the notes indicated by continuously hammering on and pulling off.

TAPPING: Hammer ("tap") the fret indicated with the pick-hand index or middle finger and pull off to the note fretted by the fret hand.

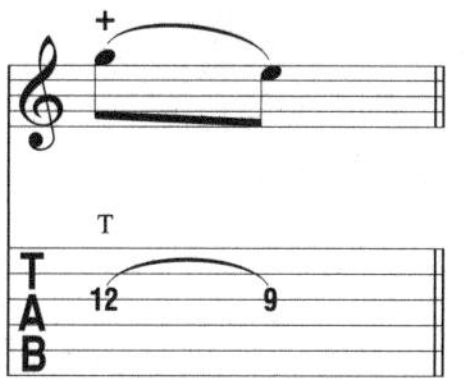

NATURAL HARMONIC: Strike the note while the fret-hand lightly touches the string directly over the fret indicated.

PINCH HARMONIC: The note is fretted normally and a harmonic is produced by adding the edge of the thumb or the tip of the index finger of the pick hand to the normal pick attack.

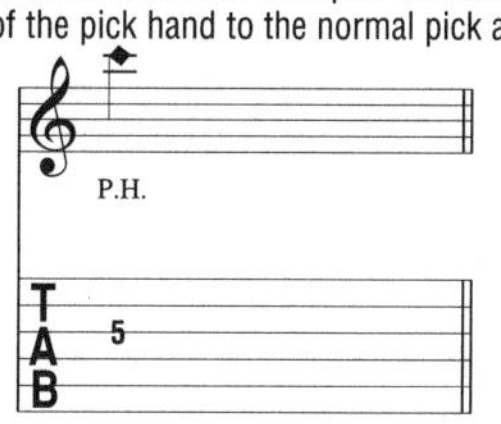

PICK SCRAPE: The edge of the pick is rubbed down (or up) the string, producing a scratchy sound.

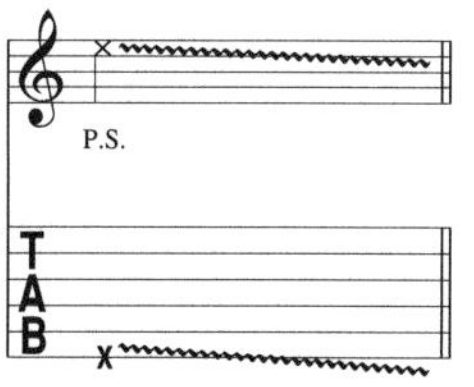

MUFFLED STRINGS: A percussive sound is produced by laying the fret hand across the string(s) without depressing, and striking them with the pick hand.

PALM MUTING: The note is partially muted by the pick hand lightly touching the string(s) just before the bridge.

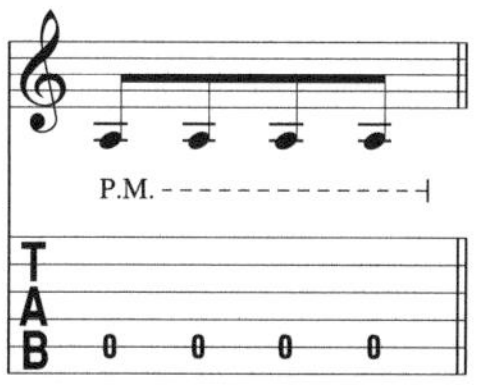

RAKE: Drag the pick across the strings indicated with a single motion.

TREMOLO PICKING: The note is picked as rapidly and continuously as possible.

VIBRATO BAR DIVE AND RETURN: The pitch of the note or chord is dropped a specified number of steps (in rhythm), then returned to the original pitch.

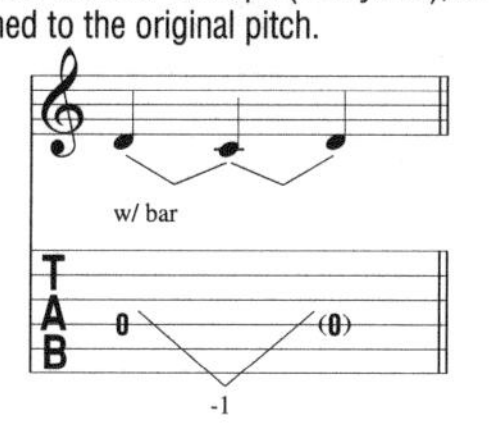

VIBRATO BAR SCOOP: Depress the bar just before striking the note, then quickly release the bar.

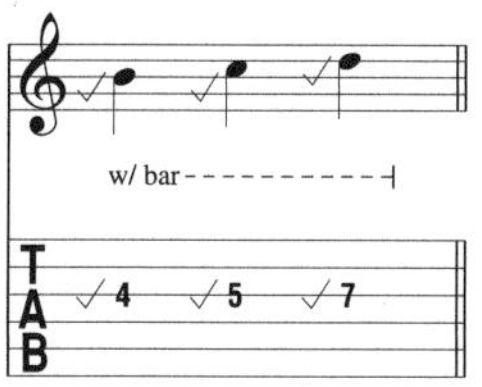

VIBRATO BAR DIP: Strike the note and then immediately drop a specified number of steps, then release back to the original pitch.

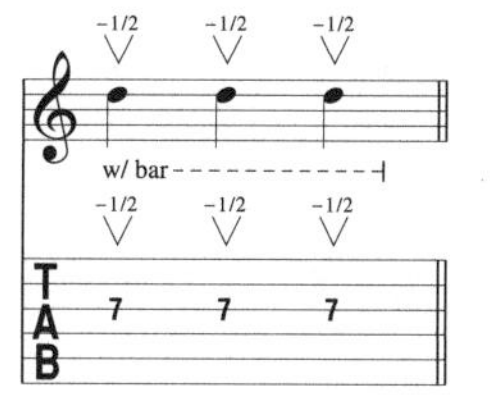

PAT METHENY COLLECTIONS

PAT METHENY – BRIGHT SIZE LIFE

INCLUDES TAB Note-for-note guitar transcriptions (carefully reviewed and approved by Metheny himself!) for all 8 songs from his highly acclaimed 1975 studio debut – which also features one of the earliest recordings of bass legend Jaco Pastorius. Includes: Bright Size Life • Midwestern Nights Dream • Missouri Uncompromised • Omaha Celebration • Round Trip/Broadway Blues • Sirabhorn • Uniquity Road • Unity Village. Contains jazz-style handwritten notation and tablature, a full-page photo of Metheny, and a Guitar Notation Legend.

00690562 Guitar Recorded Versions.................... $19.95

PAT METHENY – DAY TRIP/TOKYO DAY TRIP

INCLUDES TAB Transcriptions to all the tracks from Metheny's 2008 one-day-long recording session with bassist Christian McBride and drummer Antonio Sanchez, plus five tracks recorded live in Tokyo, including: At Last You're Here • Black Arm & Black Charge • Calvin's Keys • Day Trip • Dreaming Trees • Inori • Is This America? • Let's Move • The Night Becomes You • The Red One • Snova • Son of Thirteen • Traveling Fast • Troms0 • When We Were Free.

00691073 Guitar Recorded Versions $22.99

PAT METHENY GUITAR WARM-UPS

Ever wonder how jazz guitar great Pat Metheny could be so creative and unpredictable? Take a lesson from your hero with these original warm-ups from the man himself. This collection of 14 guitar etudes will help you to limber up, improve picking technique, and build finger independence.

00696587 .... $15.99

PAT METHENY – ONE QUIET NIGHT

INCLUDES TAB All 12 songs from the 2003 acoustic guitar recording by Metheny: Another Chance • Don't Know Why • Ferry 'Cross the Mersey • I Will Find the Way • Last Train Home • My Song • North to South, East to West • One Quiet Night • Over on 4th Street • Peace Memory • Song for the Boys • Time Goes On.

00690646 Guitar Recorded Versions $19.95

PAT METHENY – ORCHESTRION

The Complete Score

Metheny says, "'Orchestrionics' is the term that I am using to describe a method of developing ensemble-oriented music using acoustic and acoustoelectric musical instruments that are mechanically controlled in a variety of ways ... with the pieces on this particular recording leaning toward the compositional side of the spectrum. On top of these layers of acoustic sound, I add my conventional electric guitar playing as an improvised component." Here are the original scores for the five compositions: Entry Point • Expansion • Orchestrion • Soul Search • Spirit of the Air.

00001339 Scores.................................... $19.99

PAT METHENY – QUESTION AND ANSWER

INCLUDES TAB Note-for-note transcriptions with tab, in a handwritten jazz-style font and supervised by Metheny himself. Includes all the songs from this 1989 album that the All Music Guide describes as "nine tracks of sheer jazz joy," calling Pat's playing "modernistic, highly fluid, almost liquid lightning." Songs: All the Things You Are • Change of Heart • H & H • Law Years • Never Too Far Away • Old Folks • Question & Answer • Solar • Three Flights Up.

00690559 Guitar Recorded Versions $19.95

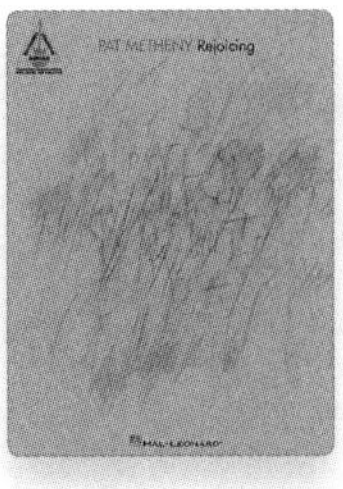

PAT METHENY – REJOICING

INCLUDES TAB Matching folio to the 1983 recording which *The All Music Guide* calls "an excellent set of memorable and unpredictable music." Includes 8 songs: Blues for Pat • The Calling • Humpty Dumpty • Lonely Woman • Rejoicing • Story from a Stranger • Tears Inside • Waiting for an Answer.

00690565 Guitar Recorded Versions . . . $19.95

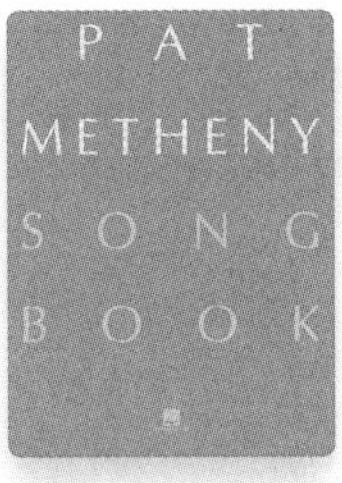

PAT METHENY SONGBOOK

This amazing book is a complete collection of lead sheets for every song this revered and prolific guitarist/composer has ever written. This comprehensive tribute features: a two-page time line of Pat Metheny milestones; a biography; a complete full-color discography including album covers, musician credits and commentary from Metheny (including his thoughts on composing, improvising, and developing a unique style); and more! There are 167 songs in all!

00660000 Lead Sheets $49.99

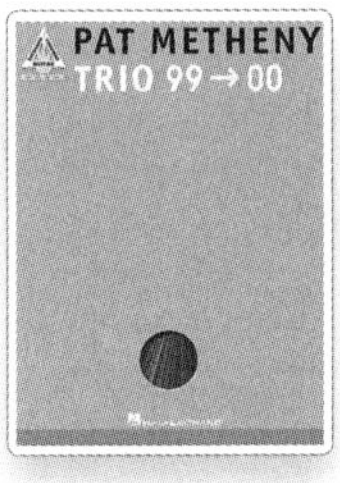

PAT METHENY – TRIO 99-00

INCLUDES TAB All 11 tracks from the 2000 release by Metheny, playing in a trio with bassist Larry Grenadier and drummer Bill Stewart. Includes: Capricorn • Giant Steps • A Lot of Livin' to Do • The Sun in Montreal • What Do You Want? • and more.

00690558 Guitar Recorded Versions $19.95

PAT METHENY TRIO – LIVE

INCLUDES TAB 13 selections from the release documenting the Trio's 2000 world tour: All the Things You Are • The Bat • Counting Texas • Faith Healer • Giant Steps • Into the Dream • James • Night Turns into Day • Soul Cowboy • Unity Village • and more.

00690561 Guitar Recorded Versions $22.95

PAT METHENY GROUP – THE WAY UP

This is the complete score for the four-part composition from this new release by the Pat Metheny Group. NPR says the album has "an ambitious compositional style that amounts to an epic journey."

00672541 Transcribed Scores............ $19.95

RECORDED VERSIONS®

The Best Note-For-Note Transcriptions Available

RECORDED VERSIONS GUITAR®

AUTHENTIC TRANSCRIPTIONS WITH NOTES AND TABLATURE

14037551 AC/DC – Backtracks $32.99
00692015 Aerosmith – Greatest Hits $22.95
00690178 Alice in Chains – Acoustic $19.95
00694865 Alice in Chains – Dirt $19.95
00690812 All American Rejects – Move Along $19.95
00690958 Duane Allman Guitar Anthology $24.99
00694932 Allman Brothers Band – Volume 1 $24.95
00694933 Allman Brothers Band – Volume 2 $24.95
00694934 Allman Brothers Band – Volume 3 $24.95
00690865 Atreyu – A Deathgrip on Yesterday $19.95
00690609 Audioslave $19.95
00690820 Avenged Sevenfold – City of Evil $24.95
00691065 Avenged Sevenfold – Waking the Fallen $22.99
00690503 Beach Boys – Very Best of $19.95
00690489 Beatles – 1 $24.99
00694832 Beatles – For Acoustic Guitar $22.99
00691014 Beatles Rock Band $34.99
00694914 Beatles – Rubber Soul $22.99
00694863 Beatles – Sgt. Pepper's Lonely Hearts Club Band $22.99
00110193 Beatles – Tomorrow Never Knows $22.99
00690110 Beatles – White Album (Book 1) $19.95
00691043 Jeff Beck – Wired $19.99
00692385 Chuck Berry $19.95
00690835 Billy Talent $19.95
00690901 Best of Black Sabbath $19.95
00690831 blink-182 – Greatest Hits $19.95
00690913 Boston $19.95
00690932 Boston – Don't Look Back $19.99
00690491 David Bowie – Best of $19.95
00690873 Breaking Benjamin – Phobia $19.95
00690451 Jeff Buckley – Collection $24.95
00690957 Bullet for My Valentine – Scream Aim Fire $22.99
00691159 The Cars – Complete Greatest Hits $22.99
00691079 Best of Johnny Cash $22.99
00690590 Eric Clapton – Anthology $29.95
00690415 Clapton Chronicles – Best of Eric Clapton $18.95
00690936 Eric Clapton – Complete Clapton $29.99
00690074 Eric Clapton – The Cream of Clapton $24.95
00694869 Eric Clapton – Unplugged $22.95
00690162 The Clash – Best of $19.95
00101916 Eric Church – Chief $22.99
00690828 Coheed & Cambria – Good Apollo I'm Burning Star, IV, Vol. 1: From Fear Through the Eyes of Madness $19.95
00691188 Coldplay – Mylo Xyloto $22.99
00690593 Coldplay – A Rush of Blood to the Head $19.95
00690819 Creedence Clearwater Revival – Best of $22.95
00690648 The Very Best of Jim Croce $19.95
00690613 Crosby, Stills & Nash – Best of $22.95
00691171 Cry of Love – Brother $22.99
00690967 Death Cab for Cutie – Narrow Stairs $22.99
00690289 Deep Purple – Best of $19.99
00690784 Def Leppard – Best of $19.95
00692240 Bo Diddley $19.99
00690347 The Doors – Anthology $22.95
00690348 The Doors – Essential Guitar Collection $16.95
14041903 Bob Dylan for Guitar Tab $19.99
00691186 Evanescence $22.99
00691181 Five Finger Death Punch – American Capitalist $22.99
00690664 Fleetwood Mac – Best of $19.95
00690870 Flyleaf $19.95
00690931 Foo Fighters – Echoes, Silence, Patience & Grace $19.95
00690808 Foo Fighters – In Your Honor $19.95
00691115 Foo Fighters – Wasting Light $22.99
00690805 Robben Ford – Best of $22.99
00694920 Free – Best of $19.95
00691050 Glee Guitar Collection $19.99
00690943 The Goo Goo Dolls – Greatest Hits Volume 1: The Singles $22.95
00113073 Green Day – ¡Uno! $21.99
00116846 Green Day – ¡Dos! $21.99
00118259 Green Day – ¡Tré! $21.99
00701764 Guitar Tab White Pages – Play-Along $39.99
00694854 Buddy Guy – Damn Right, I've Got the Blues $19.95
00690840 Ben Harper – Both Sides of the Gun $19.95
00694798 George Harrison – Anthology $19.95
00690841 Scott Henderson – Blues Guitar Collection $19.95
00692930 Jimi Hendrix – Are You Experienced? $24.95
00692931 Jimi Hendrix – Axis: Bold As Love $22.95
00692932 Jimi Hendrix – Electric Ladyland $24.95
00690017 Jimi Hendrix – Live at Woodstock $24.95
00690602 Jimi Hendrix – Smash Hits $24.99
00691152 West Coast Seattle Boy: The Jimi Hendrix Anthology $29.99
00691332 Jimi Hendrix – Winterland (Highlights) $22.99
00690793 John Lee Hooker Anthology $24.99
00690692 Billy Idol – Very Best of $19.95
00690688 Incubus – A Crow Left of the Murder $19.95
00690790 Iron Maiden Anthology $24.99
00690684 Jethro Tull – Aqualung $19.95
00690959 John5 – Requiem $22.95
00690814 John5 – Songs for Sanity $19.95
00690751 John5 – Vertigo $19.95
00690846 Jack Johnson and Friends – Sing-A-Longs and Lullabies for the Film Curious George $19.95
00690271 Robert Johnson – New Transcriptions $24.95
00699131 Janis Joplin – Best of $19.95
00690427 Judas Priest – Best of $22.99
00120814 Killswitch Engage – Disarm the Descent $22.99
00694903 Kiss – Best of $24.95
00690355 Kiss – Destroyer $16.95
00690834 Lamb of God – Ashes of the Wake $19.95
00690875 Lamb of God – Sacrament $19.95
00690823 Ray LaMontagne – Trouble $19.95
00690679 John Lennon – Guitar Collection $19.95
00690781 Linkin Park – Hybrid Theory $22.95
00690743 Los Lonely Boys $19.95
00690720 Lostprophets – Start Something $19.95
00114563 The Lumineers $22.99
00690955 Lynyrd Skynyrd – All-Time Greatest Hits $19.99
00694954 Lynyrd Skynyrd – New Best of $19.95
00690754 Marilyn Manson – Lest We Forget $19.95
00694956 Bob Marley– Legend $19.95
00694945 Bob Marley– Songs of Freedom $24.95
00690657 Maroon5 – Songs About Jane $19.95
00120080 Don McLean – Songbook $19.95
00694951 Megadeth – Rust in Peace $22.95
00691185 Megadeth – Th1rt3en $22.99
00690951 Megadeth – United Abominations $22.99
00690505 John Mellencamp – Guitar Collection $19.95
00690646 Pat Metheny – One Quiet Night $19.95
00690558 Pat Metheny – Trio: 99>00 $19.95
00690040 Steve Miller Band – Young Hearts $19.95
00102591 Wes Montgomery Guitar Anthology $24.99
00691070 Mumford & Sons – Sigh No More $22.99
00694883 Nirvana – Nevermind $19.95
00690026 Nirvana – Unplugged in New York $19.95
00690807 The Offspring – Greatest Hits $19.95
00694847 Ozzy Osbourne – Best of $22.95
00690399 Ozzy Osbourne – Ozzman Cometh $22.99
00690933 Best of Brad Paisley $22.95
00690995 Brad Paisley – Play: The Guitar Album $24.99
00694855 Pearl Jam – Ten $22.99
00690439 A Perfect Circle – Mer De Noms $19.95
00690499 Tom Petty – Definitive Guitar Collection $19.95
00690428 Pink Floyd – Dark Side of the Moon $19.95
00690789 Poison – Best of $19.95
00694975 Queen – Greatest Hits $24.95
00690670 Queensryche – Very Best of $19.95
00690878 The Raconteurs – Broken Boy Soldiers $19.95
00109303 Radiohead Guitar Anthology $24.99
00694910 Rage Against the Machine $19.95
00690055 Red Hot Chili Peppers – Blood Sugar Sex Magik $19.95
00690584 Red Hot Chili Peppers – By the Way $19.95
00691166 Red Hot Chili Peppers – I'm with You $22.99
00690852 Red Hot Chili Peppers –Stadium Arcadium $24.95
00690511 Django Reinhardt – Definitive Collection $19.95
00690779 Relient K – MMHMM $19.95
00690631 Rolling Stones – Guitar Anthology $27.95
00694976 Rolling Stones – Some Girls $22.95
00690264 The Rolling Stones – Tattoo You $19.95
00690685 David Lee Roth – Eat 'Em and Smile $19.95
00690942 David Lee Roth and the Songs of Van Halen $19.95
00690031 Santana's Greatest Hits $19.95
00690566 Scorpions – Best of $22.95
00690604 Bob Seger – Guitar Collection $19.95
00690803 Kenny Wayne Shepherd Band – Best of $19.95
00690968 Shinedown – The Sound of Madness $22.99
00122218 Skillet – Rise $22.99
00690813 Slayer – Guitar Collection $19.95
00120004 Steely Dan – Best of $24.95
00694921 Steppenwolf – Best of $22.95
00690655 Mike Stern – Best of $19.95
00690877 Stone Sour – Come What(ever) May $19.95
00690520 Styx Guitar Collection $19.95
00120081 Sublime $19.95
00120122 Sublime – 40oz. to Freedom $19.95
00690929 Sum 41 – Underclass Hero $19.95
00690767 Switchfoot – The Beautiful Letdown $19.95
00690993 Taylor Swift – Fearless $22.99
00115957 Taylor Swift – Red $21.99
00690531 System of a Down – Toxicity $19.95
00694824 James Taylor – Best of $17.99
00690871 Three Days Grace – One-X $19.95
00690683 Robin Trower – Bridge of Sighs $19.95
00699191 U2 – Best of: 1980-1990 $19.95
00690732 U2 – Best of: 1990-2000 $19.95
00660137 Steve Vai – Passion & Warfare $24.95
00110385 Steve Vai – The Story of Light $22.99
00690116 Stevie Ray Vaughan – Guitar Collection $24.95
00660058 Stevie Ray Vaughan – Lightnin' Blues 1983-1987 $24.95
00694835 Stevie Ray Vaughan – The Sky Is Crying $22.95
00690015 Stevie Ray Vaughan – Texas Flood $19.95
00690772 Velvet Revolver – Contraband $22.95
00690071 Weezer (The Blue Album) $19.95
00690966 Weezer – (Red Album) $19.99
00690447 The Who – Best of $24.95
00690916 The Best of Dwight Yoakam $19.95
00691020 Neil Young – After the Gold Rush $22.99
00691019 Neil Young – Everybody Knows This Is Nowhere $19.99
00691021 Neil Young – Harvest Moon $22.99
00690905 Neil Young – Rust Never Sleeps $19.99
00690623 Frank Zappa – Over-Nite Sensation $22.99
00690589 ZZ Top Guitar Anthology $24.95

FOR A COMPLETE LIST OF GUITAR RECORDED VERSIONS TITLES, SEE YOUR LOCAL MUSIC DEALER, OR WRITE TO:

HAL•LEONARD® CORPORATION

7777 W. BLUEMOUND RD. P.O. BOX 13819 MILWAUKEE, WI 53213

Visit Hal Leonard online at
www.halleonard.com

Prices and availability subject to change without notice.
Some products may not be available outside the U.S.A.

1113

TAB+

Accurate Tabs
Gear Information
Selected Pedal Settings
Analysis & Playing Tips

The Tab+ Series gives you note-for-note accurate transcriptions in notes and tab PLUS a whole lot more. These books also include performance notes to help you master the song, tips on the essential gear to make the song sound its best, recording techniques, historical information, right- and left-hand techniques and other playing tips – it's all here!

TAB. TONE. TECHNIQUE.

25 TOP ACOUSTIC SONGS

Big Yellow Taxi • Can't Find My Way Home • Cat's in the Cradle • The Clap • Closer to the Heart • Free Fallin' • Going to California • Good Riddance (Time of Your Life) • Hey There Delilah • A Horse with No Name • I Got a Name • Into the Mystic • Lola • Losing My Religion • Love the One You're With • Never Going Back Again • Norwegian Wood (This Bird Has Flown) • Ooh La La • Patience • She Talks to Angels • Shower the People • Tequila Sunrise • The Weight • Wild Horses • Wish You Were Here.

00109283 .... $19.99

25 TOP CLASSIC ROCK SONGS

Addicted to Love • After Midnight • Another Brick in the Wall, Part 2 • Aqualung • Beat It • Brown Sugar • China Grove • Domino • Dream On • For What It's Worth • Fortunate Son • Go Your Own Way • Had to Cry Today • Keep Your Hands to Yourself • Life in the Fast Lane • Lights • Message in a Bottle • Peace of Mind • Reeling in the Years • Refugee • Rock and Roll Never Forgets • Roundabout • Tom Sawyer • Up on Cripple Creek • Wild Night.

00102519 .... $19.99

25 TOP HARD ROCK SONGS

Back in Black • Best of Both Worlds • Crazy Train • Detroit Rock City • Doctor, Doctor • Fire Woman • Hair of the Dog • In My Dreams • In-A-Gadda-Da-Vida • Jailbreak • Nobody's Fool • Paranoid • Rock Candy • Rock of Ages • School's Out • Shout at the Devil • Smoke on the Water • Still of the Night • Stone Cold • Welcome to the Jungle • Whole Lotta Love • Working Man • You've Got Another Thing Comin' • Youth Gone Wild • The Zoo.

00102469 .... $19.99

25 TOP METAL SONGS

Ace of Spades • Afterlife • Am I Evil? • Blackout • Breaking the Law • Chop Suey! • Cowboys from Hell • Down with the Sickness • Evil • Freak on a Leash • Hangar 18 • Iron Man • Laid to Rest • The Last in Line • Madhouse • Mr. Crowley • Psychosocial • Pull Me Under • Raining Blood • Roots Bloody Roots • Sober • Tears Don't Fall • Thunder Kiss '65 • The Trooper • Unsung.

00102501 .... $19.99

25 TOP POST-GRUNGE SONGS

All Star • Bawitdaba • Blurry • Boulevard of Broken Dreams • Bring Me to Life • Closing Time • Devour • Du Hast • Everlong • Far Behind • Hero • How You Remind Me • I Hate Everything About You • I Stand Alone • It's Been Awhile • Kryptonite • Metalingus • My Own Summer (Shove It) • One Last Breath • One Week • The Reason • Remedy • Sex and Candy • Thnks Fr Th Mmrs • Wish You Were Here.

00102518...................................... $19.99

HAL•LEONARD®
CORPORATION
7777 W. BLUEMOUND RD. P.O. BOX 13819
MILWAUKEE, WISCONSIN 53213

www.halleonard.com

Prices, contents, and availability subject to change without notice.